The Little Gift Book of
BULGARIA

ODYSSEIA - IN TRAVEL

www.odysseia-in.com; www.UniqueBulgaria.com
E-mail: odysseia@omega.bg; tel.: 000359 2 989 05 38

The Little Gift Book of
BULGARIA

BORINA

First published in Bulgaria in 2004
by Borina Publishing House

E-mail: borina@borina.com
www.borina.com

ISBN 954 500 114 3

Printed in the Czech Republic

Nature that has something of everything, with signs left from all ages: if you are looking for this, Bulgaria is the right place. Hardly are there so many lands in the world that on such an easily traversed space you can have – even within the frame of a single day – both magnificent seaside and hospitable mountains with fine white snow-capped summits; to travel through cloughs that make you dizzy, through staggering canyons and gorges, enraptured by swift-running rivers with wondrous waterfalls, by secluded caves and azure lakes… However hard you may try to check the speed fascinated by the wonderful sights, yet they will change before your eyes with an unbelievable swiftness as there are something of everything, both from the north and from the south; from the quiet plain down there and from the steep slopes and cliffs; from the naked empty ridges and the boundless deciduous and coniferous forests… For the connoisseurs of the authentic and genuine there are scores of protected natural areas and architectural reserves; for the inquisitive eye there are matchless finds hardly occurring elsewhere; for those that look for enjoyment and delight there are opportunities that here were traditionally offered to gods.

As a crossroad of the world civilisations during the last ten millennia that the eye can span, from a field for all sorts of historical adventures, Bulgaria has become the land of tolerance and dialogue between different ethnic communities and religions. Only a people quick on the uptake, adaptive and combinative, open to the outside world, hospitable to those crossing its land, patient with intruders and wise in the selection and preservation of the archetypal and most enduring of its values.

Here, you can not only find traces from all the past ages, here you can live simultaneously in at least 30 centuries for the journey around Bulgaria is not a transition from ancient to medieval monuments but – as the famous Russian academician Dmitry Likhachov has aptly termed it - 'a sojourn in the State of Spirit'.

It was remembered until 1585 that the lands of today's Bulgaria have 'given birth' to Europe. And the still living until then tradition had been documented not here but in the northernmost lands of the continent. And in an exceptionally original way at that: on a map of Thrace created in Holland by Abraham Ortelius the space between Apollonia Magna (today's Sozopol), Constantinople (today's Istanbul in Turkey) and Phillippopolis (today's Plovdiv) was named … the Province of Europe.

These lands have been inhabited since the most ancient times. The first identified tribes in the distant past that still can be examined by us were the forefathers of the Thracians. The expand dominated by them spans the lands from the Carpathian Mountains in the north down to today's Greece and Peloponnesus together with the northern islands in the Aegean Sea in the south and from the Black Sea in the east to the rivers of Morava and Vardar in the west. With their ethnic name of Thracians they were famous even before the 13th century BC. Moreover, by that time they had already populated Asia Minor where they also had founded petty states of their own. Seven centuries later Herodotus wrote about them that they "are the most numerous people on earth after the Hindus". He had also noted that if they were to be ruled by a single Tsar they could have easily conquered the world. But they were divided into many tribes: Geti, Mysi, Tribali, Sigini, Odrisi, Asti, Uzdikenzi, Obulenzi, Terizi, Tilatei, Serdi, Velikokoylaleti, Seleti, Nipsei, Tini, Melanofagi, Diobesi, Satri, Frigi, Malokoyalaleti, Medi, Vitini, Sinti, Kikoni, Sapei, Korpili, Bisalti, Migdoni, Edoni, Dolonki, etc. This is not simply a territorial differentiation and isolation – each one of these tribes has been famous with its own specific virtues: Geti were much more bellicose, Besi were much more mystically inclined, Odrisi were pronouncedly artistic, Mysi – more diplomatic with foreigners… Thus was born not only the rich cultural heritage of the unbelievably divers material monuments that have remained here but since the most remote past the amazing peculiarities in the spiritual culture of each region had been predetermined. These peculiarities are preserved today in the folklore, traditional folk costumes and in the rites of the calendar custom related with the still not forgotten ecclesiastic practices.

Here one can trace out how the European civilisation was born. Throughout Bulgaria one can see the first by time architectural monuments – the vertically erected stone columns in the Thracians' shrines. They were usually located on high rocky summits and many of them were ancient astronomical observatories called by the old locals 'preslap'. There are scores of such sites throughout Bulgaria but two of these will suffice to give an example: at one of them, close to the village of Zhelezare, region of Plovdiv, the erected stones have a height of 2.20 m and are arranged in a circle with a diameter of 7 m, while near the village of Dolni Glavanak, at a distance of 60 km from the city of Kardzhali the upright fixed stone blocks are 1.5 m to 1.8 m high while the circle outlined by them has internal diameter of about 12 m.

Among the earliest manifestations of conscious, intentional building activity dated 4th through 2nd millennium BC are the dolmens erected of huge stone plates, thus being the first purposefully fenced off and covered areas. Only on a relatively small tract of the land of three villages in the Mount Sakar - namely Balgarska Polyana, Sakartsi and Hlyabovo – one can see such a diversity of dolmens that one can get the notion of their evolution on a global scale! And the same forms of dolmens consisting of a chamber and an anteroom are repeated in the rocky massif in Rodopi Mountains, in the vicinity of the town of Provadia, Region of Varna as well as on the northern Black Sea Coast…

The in-mound temples dated between the 5th and the 4th centuries BC can be regarded as gates linking this world with the world beyond. They are the next stage in the development of the art of building. The in-mound temples can be divided into three types depending on the construction of the covering on chambers: those with round chambers covered with a 'false' dome; the other type, with square chambers covered by the same principle by cross-diagonally fixed stone plates that are brought together at the top; and still other type with square chambers again but cylindrically arcaded on top. Apart from being used for pilgrimage and for performing the posthumous rites by the mortal remains of noble deceased, these temples were used for holding the special services of the first esoteric male societies related with death and the overcoming of death – topics that were most often manifested in the artistic and sculptural decoration of the chambers.

More than 150,000 mounds (or knolls) made by Thracians in the course of 3.5 millennia stand in today's Bulgarian lands and in many of them in-mound temples are still hidden. They are amazing both with that every next one is a yet unseen creation with its wondrously nice columns, with its monolithic construction and its exquisite friezes but also with their solidity. In some of them, like the Kazanlak and the Aleksandrovo knolls, what captivates the imagination of visitors is the wall painted decorations, while in the chambers of others, like those at Sveshtari and Starosel for instance, triumph the purely architectural motifs carved out of stone. The images painted on their vaults look so alive, and this by itself is an evidence of the great artistry of the painters. Though they have stayed at least 3000 years buried under the ground the frescoes have not lost the many colours with which they were executed because the manufacturers of paints possessed extremely good knowledge about the substances they used in the process of producing paints as well as the coating on which they were laid. This is the reason why in the loveliest one, the Aleksandrovo mound, the fresco painter had insisted on placing his signature: 'Kodzimases Chrestos'. And besides has left his self-portrait, the oldest one on the continent – since before 24 centuries!

The first documented resurrection is also related with these lands and took place almost five centuries before Christ raised Lazarus from the dead. Herodotus describes a demonstration performed by the Tsar of the Thracians-Geti Zalmoksis: after a ritual feast with selected people at which, according to his custom he preached to them saying death would not reign over them, he entered a vault, built especially and purposefully for him where he remained buried for three years. "On the fourth year he appeared again before them and thus they believed in what he used to tell them" ends his story the 'father of history'.
Just after he met Zalmoksis Pythagoras adopted the idea of immortality and introduced it into the ancient Greek philosophy. You can enter into the mystical world of the Thracians-Geti even today when you visit the historical and archaeological reserve 'Sboryanovo' near the town of Isperih, region of Razgrad.

The first secret male community was set up in the second half of the 2nd millennium BC in the Rodopi Mountains by Orpheus, the Tsar-High Priest of the Thracians-Besi. Living among a people who used to hold in esteem and celebrate his deities with wine, feasts and dances of maenads, these predecessors of the future mystical orders devoted themselves to mysteries involving prolonged fasting, vegetarianism, refraining from drinking alcohol and shunning women. Such preliminary privations were necessary as the initiated were to proceed with the essential part of the service by drinking kikeon (a special beverage made of baked barley grains stirred in honey water spiced with peppermint) and inhaled the white smoke from herbs they threw in the fire before them, and both these agents affected only people that had undergone a long fast. The impact was further exalted by the special hymns they sang together with Orpheus and in this way achieved ecstasy and, while in this state, divine revelations.
Part of the secret in which these noble men were initiated made them to order special niches to be

hewn in the cliffs of Rodopi Mountains where their relics were to be left after their death instead of in tombs or vaults so that during the day the sun would shine on them while in the night they would be lit by the light of stars. The urn with the mortal remains of Orpheus was put on a tall column in order to be at equal distance both from the earth and from heavens.

At several sites in Bulgaria's lands of today: near the village of Gradeshnitsa, region of Varna, near the village of Karanovo, district of Nova Zagora, among the ruins of the sacred for the Thracians Perperikon, in the lands of the Besi in the vicinity of today's city of Kardzhali, etc., archaeologists have found clay plates with letters dated as far back as the 4th millennium BC. All of these plates have been recognised as a scientific sensation as the letters were found to be older than the oldest known ones - that from the island of Crete. These letters are a firm evidence that the culture of the people that inhabited these lands does not give in to the civilisations of Asia Minor, the Near East and Egypt, and that the Balkan Peninsula was one of the centres of the most highly developed ancient civilisations. Unfortunately no one has yet succeeded in deciphering the texts. Possibly it was a sacred script for the Thracians as for their everyday needs they used the Greek alphabet.

Thracians were the first metalworkers on the European continent: they were known to produce copper as early as 8000 years ago. They developed the oldest copper mine in Europe, the one located in the countryside area called 'Mechi Kladenets' (the Bears' Well) in the region of the city of Stara Zagora. So far 6 of the mining developments have been traced out down to a depth of 18 m. Archaeologists have found traces from the oldest metallurgy in Europe dated back to the 6th millennium BC (i.e. 20 centuries before anywhere else on the continent) in an early Neolithic family dwelling, excavated near the village of Yabalkovo not far from the town of Dimitrovgrad. Soon the Thracians started mining iron from the rich ore deposits in mountains of their lands, so that in the period of 8th through 6th century BC they already manufactured their weapons and tools from it.

The oldest articles made of tooled gold in Europe were found in a village hillock 'Hotnitsa' not far from the city of Veliko Tarnovo. They were dated 4300 BC and served as cult and rites articles. Most of them are compositions of rings linked to form necklaces and lamellae showing heavily stylised human images. And in a necropolis located on the northern shore of Varna lake 3100 gold objects of total weight over 6.5 kg were found, among which were the earliest symbols of power: two gold sceptres, an indisputable evidence for the emergence of the ruler's institution. The so far studied 300 burials were dated by the end of the 5th millennium BC and experts believe that discoveries are yet to come as most of the seaside settlements of that earliest European civilisation have sunk under water. There are no other ancient peoples, who have buried its dead with so many gold presents and who have left so many treasures in the earth as donations to their gods. Invaluable specimens of these can be seen in every more or less important historical museum in Bulgaria.

Apart from having here the first and richest gold and silver mines of the antiquity, today's Bulgarian lands have preserved the oldest gold mine as well. It can be seen in the Rodopi Mountains, near today's village of Stremtsi. Some ten entrances into the mine and more than 500 m of drifts have so far been excavated and preserved. The most precious Byzantine medieval coin, the 22-carats 'hyperperon' or better known as 'perpera' is related with this mine. 'Perpera' is named after the sacred for the Thracians Perperikon, which is located at only 2 km away from the mine. Later, a large part of the drifts was intentionally flooded – perhaps because treasures were hidden in them in perilous for the Thracians times.

The oldest facemasks were found in the same necropolis near Varna that was mentioned above. There, graves with symbolic burials were excavated, in which the 'buried' was represented only with his/her unique mask made of unburned clay. A gold plate is put in the place of the mouth with gold nails under it; ears are marked with several gold earrings; on the brow lies a gold diadem, and instead of the eyes there are round gold plates. The neck is decorated with anthropomorphic amulets, also made of gold. Initially, these masks were unintentionally formed - by smearing (i.e. anointing) faces of the deceased ones with clay to demonstrate that the dead have passed into another world and have nothing to do with the previous occupants of these bodies anymore. These masks were called 'christos' for that meant 'a substance that serves to smear, or anoint, with', [the name of our Lord Christ derives from that word and means 'the Anointed One (by God)']. Later, Thracians began placing specially made silver masks on the faces of the diseased. Participants in some of the rites devoted to the Thracian gods Sabasius, Zagrey, Dionysus also wore facemasks…
Ancient Greeks liked the scenes performed by participants in those rites and began to stage their own theatrical performance after the Thracian model. According to the Thracian custom the actors had to wear masks on their faces to demonstrate that they have already become different persons, characters in a drama.

Deep in the antiquity Thracian rulers had their own castles. The ancient Greek authors describe them as 'tursis' which means 'tower' because the strongholds were conspicuous by their height. Naturally, it was out of question to regard them as simple fortress' towers because the ruler has with himself a numerous armed guards and they were due garrison premises with outhouses for the horses, food stores, carts, etc. Besides, these were not housed in the citadel of the main strongholds (called 'diza', while those in the big fortified towns were called 'bria'), where the seats of the tribal chieftains and aristocracy were but used to build settlements outside the town limits for them – near famous shrines and in the border areas of the state where the Tsar used to stay for some time during his obligatory annual inspection tours.
Remains of the 'turses' can be seen at many places in today's Bulgaria but the sacred town of Perperikon made quite a stir in recent times. It is located near the present-day city of Kardzhali in the Eastern Rodopi Mountains. The palace was built by the mythical Thracians at least 2300 years ago. It was hewn so deep into the sacred for the Thracians rocks that at places its 'halls' have penetrated into the stone at a depth of 6 to 7 m. However, it is not a narrow 'tower' – its overall area is more than 10,000 sq.-m, with at least thirty or so separate premises on the ground floor

only! Above it the 'tower' had 3 or 4 more floors with a total of 50 or 60 halls, rooms, corridors…
The access to the palace was via a 100-m long approach, up to 4 m wide, also cut into the rock that
raises above it up to 7 or 8 m at places.
Apart from this palace being fenced in with a thick stone wall, there is an acropolis above it with a
separate fortified wall up to 2.8 m thick. In the centre of this 'upper town' there also was a palace but
it resembled much more a tower – 'only' 7 rooms were found in its ground floor.

The shrine of god Dionysus from 18th-17th century BC: one of the two famous oracles in the
antiquity (together with the Apollo's oracle at Delphi) is also there, above the sacred town of
Perperikon where the Thraicans-Besi, the Orpheus own tribe, worked their wonders. Amidst the
oval hall hewn in the living rock there is a stone of perfect round shape. It is heavily burnt by fire that
was lighted innumerable times there and upon which priests poured wine from a special phial. Then
they would divine by the flames into which the divine drink would blaze up. This was the reason
why the sanctuary had no roof. The oracle in the shrine of the Besi at Perperikon predicted to the
military commanders Alexander the Macedon and Gaius Julius Caesar that they would conquer the
world, testifies the father of history Herododtus.
The mysteries here were performed until 5th-6th century AD.

For millennia the ancient Greeks called the Thracians 'thallassic aristocrats', i.e. the 'sea lords
of the world'. One of the first confrontations with them took place in the 60s of the 13th century BC
during the war of Troy: Thracian warriors led by the legendary Tsar Rezos fought on the side of
Trojans who were their blood relatives.
The other 'world wars' waged by the Thracians were related with the famous Persian Tsar Darius I
whom they fought in 493 and 492 BC and with Tsar Phillip II the Macedon who fell upon them in
the middle of the 4th century BC. In 335 his son Alexander the Macedon resumed the war. On the part
of the Thracians-Geti their prince Dromihet captured Alexander's heir Lysimachus and took him to
his fortified residence Helis.
A curious detail about mythical Thracians is the following one: in 341 BC when the numerous army
of Phillip II the Macedon had laid siege to the Thracian town of Odessos (today's Varna) the gates
of the fortress suddenly opened and out came against the foe the priests from the town's temples all
dressed in white and armed with … guitars.

The great fertility of the 'fat-soil' Thracian land, with the best chernozem soils in the Balkan
Peninsula, was praised in song by the ancient singers - and it suffice just to taste the products
made from the grain, fruits and vegetables grown on this soil to know what relish and strength
they give. The fur- and pine forests of those days in the high southern mountains Rodopi,
Rila, Pirin, Strandzha were immeasurably richer than today's and the centuries-old beech and
oak forests covered much more densely the slopes of today's Stara Planina and Sredna Gora
Mountains. The coniferous trees yielded the resin, which was very much in demand at those

times, while all the forests yielded in abundance the high quality timber used as construction wood, for building houses, fortresses and ships.

This land is famed with the most proficient healers: the ancient ones wrote that it was named after the nymph Tràke who was unsurpassed in the enchantments involving herbs and incantations. They reckoned that this was the reason the Thracians to be able not only to apply in the most expertly way the invaluable curing herbs that grow on their lands but also to combine the therapy with curative seances and suggestions. Even today one can find in the wild more than 170 endemic species of plants, i.e. such that occur only in Bulgaria of the whole world.

Besides, the descendants of Tràke made the discoveries that the 'modern' European medicine managed to achieve only in 20th century AD, like this principle for instance: 'As one should not start healing the eyes without healing the entire body, so one should not start healing the body without healing at the same time the soul.' This fame was the reason why the Thracian healers were the most sought ones in their time and, consequently, why they were the richest.

The ancient Greeks knew the Thracians best because not only they invaded and gradually occupied Peloponnesus and the port towns along the Aegean coast but with the passing of time succeeded to persuade the Thracian Tsars to give them the Black Sea coastal towns for which to pay taxes. The Hellenes liked not only Thracian mysteries and rites, but they also borrowed the gods of their mystical neighbours. Some of them they took right with their Thracian names, for instance the bellicose Ares, the merry and powerful Dionysus, the audacious Bendida (which the Greek re-christened in Artemis), the healer Asclepius, the god-sun Apollo, worshipped by the Orpheists, etc.

Along with the gods the Thracian myths, effigies and spirituality passed (and were preserved) in the ancient Greek culture and from it went into the Roman one (particularly after Thrace was incorporated into the Roman Empire in the 1st century AD). On a large silver phaler, or badge discovered among several others in a burial near today's Bulgarian city of Stara Zagora, there is a splendid scene with the mythical hero Hercules: it shows how he had taken a good grip around the neck of a lion and is about to slay it as he was standing between a pair of two other upright lions. Ancient Greeks loved very much to depict this scene but in their paintings the hero only suffocates the beast, as the clutch with the Thracian crescent-shaped knife called mahaira is typical for their northern neighbours. The Greeks depict the man naked, while with the Thracians the warrior had to be decently dressed.

In Leiden and in Paris archaeologists found the same images as the Thracian ones. These, however, were works of the Celts who invaded Thracian lands in 278 BC when the local tribes were exhausted by the prolonged wars waged at that time. Celts even established their own kingdom here – until they mastered some of the skills popular in Tsar Sevt III's land. Thrace assumed the role of intermediary between the East and the West and … the pair of erected lions by Hercules who slaughters a third one later decorated a lot of coats of arms throughout Europe.

The first Christian church in Europe was founded and a temple erected on Apostle Paul's suggestion by the present-day village of Ognyanovo located between the mountains of Pirin and Rodopi. As is well known, in 52 AD Apostle Paul landed near the town of Phillipi at the mouth of river Mesta and going upstream he reached the Roman town of Nicopolis ad Nestum (the remains of which can be seen at present in the area of today's Bulgarian town of Gotse Delchev).

Constantine the Great had chosen Serdica (today's Sofia) as his first Christian capital city, after Christianity was recognised and adopted as equal in rights with the other faiths in the empire by the edict of Milan of 313 AD. He leaves Rome and sets out looking for a clean place, which would suit to become the centre of Christian civilisation. *'Serdica is my Rome!'* exclaims the Emperor upon arrival in the lands of the Thracian-Serdi.

Even today, in mid-Sofia in the courtyard behind the President's Palace one can see the ruins of the buildings of the Imperial administration, from which he ruled the western part of the Roman Empire. And through the ages here and around the erection of holy buildings and places did not stop and this activity has contributed to the city becoming famous with so many monasteries around it that they were called conjointly the 'Sacred Mount of Sofia' by analogy with the Mount Athos in today's Greece.

Before setting out on their march to the West the Germans 'stocked' for quite a long time here: since their tribe 'kimberi' the lands of today's Bulgaria crossed in the 1st century BC. An evidence of the spiritual closeness they had achieved with the Thracians are the scenes depicted on the famous Thracian-German cauldron, 'Gundesdruck-kessel' from the town of Bormose, Denmark. Consequently, other old-German tribes also arrived here. Constantine the Great himself settled in 332 AD in Mysia and Thrace more than 300,000 Visigoths. In 391 AD Alarich I was elected king of the Visigoths in Thrace and from Nove (today's town of Svishtov on the Danube) in 395 AD he set out with his army towards Rome thus entering the world history as the first conqueror of Rome in 410 AD.

Again in today's Bulgarian land, about a century later, the Ostrogoth ruler Teodorich the Great (453-526 AD) ruled for 15 years in Nove. He later became also world renowned as the King of Ravena and joined the German mythology as Dietrich von Bern and the Norwegian one as Tidrik, presented today as a historical figure and a life-work in almost all west-European history textbooks.

Here bishop Vulfila (311-383 AD) translated the Bible into Gothic: by today's city of Veliko Tarnovo, which in the Middle Ages became Bulgaria's capital city (throne-abode). Near the town is what has left from the ancient Roman town of Nicopolis ad Istrum (the remnants of which can be seen today near the village of Nikyup) where the Gothic letters were invented based on the Greek alphabet and the old-German runes. Here the 'apostle' of Goths standardised the first post-antiquity European language and created the first new letters of Europe. Codex argenteus, a copy of Vulfila's Bible made much later, in the time of Teodorich the Great in Ravena, today is kept as the first significant monument of the old-German written culture in the University Library in the town of Uppsala, Sweden. Here, in the beginning of the 5th century AD the Gothic Liturgical Calendar was also invented and then used in all Gothic kingdoms.

In 681 AD Bulgarians arrive in the land of the Thracians-Geti. As a community, they are a people spiritually quite close to Thracians - worshipping the Horse and the Horseman as the Thracians did. They also have their own special, slightly crescent-like towards the point sword but curbed the other way opposite to the the curve of the Thracian knife. This was the sabre. Bulgarians were able to slash terribly with it while riding at full speed because they have invented another extremely important thing – the stirrup, on which the rider sets his foot, gets supported and thus becomes able to slash powerfully with his sabre. Bulgarians enlisted the Slav tribes – which have already liked the lands on the other side of the Danube - as their infantry; they defeated Byzantium (as the eastern part of the Roman Empire was called after it was divided into two). Thus Bulgarians founded the third in their history state called Bulgaria, the one on the Danube, in the lands of the Thracian-Odrisi.

A new translation of the Bible, this time in Slav-Bulgarian, came into being in this region of Europe in 865 AD together with the new alphabet, the one the holy equal to the apostles brothers Cyril and Methodius created, the Glagolitic alphabet.

Soon here a newer letters were born, the Cyrillic alphabet, which was invented by Cyril and Methodius' follower, Sveti Kliment (Saint Clement) and which is used today not only by Bulgarians, but by a number of other Orthodox peoples that have adopted the letters and the teaching of Christ from Bulgarians. The united spiritual energy of Thracians, Slavs, Goths and Bulgarians melted into one nation had created the medieval cultural wonder called by the Russian academician Dmitry Likhachov 'the State of Spirit'.

Not only museums and temples in Bulgaria but a number of cloisters and depositories around the world are full of its fruits.

Bulgarians are zealous followers of Christ and after their conversion to Christianity they abandoned their first capital on this side of the Danube, as Constantine the Great did before them with Rome.

That is why it is easy now to see how Bulgarians have further developed and enriched their original building traditions in conformity with the new doctrine of faith in the new capital. Particularly curious in this respect is the famous Round Church there – obviously a 'preslap' preserved forever in the appearance of a Christian temple. The place original toponym has been transformed and the capital city that emerged there was called … Preslav.

In the country surrounding Tarnovo, too, which we call today Veliko Tarnovo, Bulgarians have built a new Sveta Gora (Holy Mount) of monasteries when the town on the banks of river Yantra became the next capital of Bulgaria – exactly as it was done in the vicinity of Sofia several hundred years before. But the necklace of holy cloisters on the hills surrounding the town was not erected as a curtsy of the Tsars to the clergy: these temples and monks' cells became spiritual centres of the State in which not only philosophy and the practice of isihasmus (Greek for meditation) were thriving in 13th – 14th century but the literature of that time was also created (and of the future centuries as well) while the new spiritual leaders of the nation were raised.

The first preserved Bulgarian museum of history dates from 1230 AD. It was built by the greatest at that time Tsar in the Balkans, Ivan-Asen II, who managed to unite in a Bulgarian State almost all lands of the Thracians. The tradition of the old Bulgarian rulers was to put on stone plates and columns the important state decrees, conventions and stories about fateful historical events. As an eulogy for Bulgaria, not long before resurrected from Byzantine captivity and in memory of her over-glorious public figures the Tsar had ordered the gathering together of the famous columns with inscriptions cut on them by the orders of Khan Umortag in the beginning of the 9th century AD and adding of a column with inscriptions describing his own deeds during his reign; to this end he had to build them in a church erected near one of the entrances into the citadel Tsarevets in the capital Tarnovgrad. The temple was named 'Sveti 40 machenitsi" (The Holy 40 martyrs) and by it was established the necropolis of the Bulgarian aristocracy from 13th and 14th century.

And because it has shined through the centuries as a symbol of Bulgarian Tsardom, Tsar Ferdinand Saxe Coburg-Gotha elected to proclaim on September 22, 1908 the independence of Bulgaria (declared in 1878 as a Principality tributary to the Ottoman Empire) in this exactly church.

Neither the decision of Tsar Ivan-Asen II, nor the act of Tsar Ferdinand Saxe Coburg-Gotha was whimsical – after the tradition both of ancient Thracians and ancient Bulgarians the ruler of the State is at the same time its high priest who performs personally the most sacred rites. This is why the first Bulgarian museum emerged rightly in a temple and not in a palace hall.

The special features of the old mystical practice were not repudiated either and the traditional sacred rocks were hewn again or the caves-vaults were reconstructed, this time as rock churches and cells for 'buried alive' monks, who founded in them the rock monasteries. The fact that donors to these monks' communities in the Middle Ages were the Tsars Ivan-Asen II, Ivan-Alexander, Tsarina Theodora-Sara, and that some Tsars (like Georgi Terter I) had even abandoned their thrones and had retired in such primeval sacred places is an explicit evidence on how high in the spiritual hierarchy these new-old cloisters stood.

The tradition is alive even today: Basarbovo rock monastery is still inhabited and follows its dedicated to God services. It is one of the three existing and alive rock cloisters in the Balkan Peninsula along with the Meteora in Greece and Radozhda in Macedonia.

The spiritual energy from the sanctuaries of the ancient Thracians gushes forth at present too through the Christian temples or the Muslim teke built upon their foundations. There are sacred sites where one can trace down the history of civilisation by the buildings that stand today or once were standing there. They have overlapped in time and have succeeded each other, and have remained as sites (topos) of faith: the Orphic of the Thracians, the Tangroistic of the ancient Bulgarians, the Christian and the Muslim. There are many of them in the north, in the reserve of architecture and history Sboryanovo; there are no less of them in the south, in the biggest megalith in the Balkans, Perperek.

Building skills, developed in the course of hundreds of years on the basis of traditional styles and technologies available to the tribes and peoples that have crossed these lands triumphed until present time with the kilometres on end of preserved Roman roads in different regions of Bulgaria; with the temples 'Sveti Georgi' (4th century AD) and 'Sveta Sofia' (6th century AD) in today's Bulgarian capital; with the churches in the antique seaside towns Sozopol and Nesebar; with the castle-fortress of the Bulgarian Tsars 'Baba Vida' in the Danube town of Vidin (the tower of which was erected in 13th century AD); with the Islamic cult buildings, each one several centuries old, in the cities of Sofia, Shoumen, Samokov, Razgrad, Yambol; with the towers built of stone and used as dwellings in the town of Vratsa, in the village of Ledenik, region of Veliko Tarnovo; in several monasteries in the country and in the solemn and stern clock-towers that were erected in 18th and 19th centuries in the trade and artisan centres of the then prospering settlements…

As in these public constructions triumphs the worshipping of stone so customary for Thracians and the massive sturdy stonework executed with quadri (hewn stones of roughly cubic form), so in the two-storey houses with open verandas facing the flower gardens that Bulgarians built for their families one can definitely see the principles revealed by archaeologists in the residential construction of the Thracian capital Sevtopol (4th century BC - today on the bottom of a reservoir). During the Renaissance the number of storeys grows, the upper ones frequently jutting out as oriels and hangingover streets, while inside the rooms become increasingly better and more richly decorated with carved wooden ceilings and furniture. But behind this common model, traditional for more than 22 centuries one can see the tremendous diversity of building manner typical for every region: there are fair renaissance architectural reserves in the Stara Planina mountain towns Veliko Tarnovo, Lòvech, Teteven, Troyan, Tryavna, Gabrovo, Elena, Kotel; in the Sub-Balkan ones like Koprivshtitsa, Sopot, Karlovo; in flat Thracian plain like Plovdiv; in the bosom of Pirin Mountain like Melnik, Bansko, Razlog; and the tucked away in the Rodopi Mountains Smolyan and Zlatograd as well as on the Black Sea coast like Nesebar and Sozopol…

The successors of their builders live today in these cosy old houses. In many of them tourists can stay, and not only to have a brief respite amid their unique atmosphere but also to taste the specialities that their proprietors have cooked.

And especially blessed these lands are for making pilgrimages: there are more than 250 monasteries, many of which founded in the Middle Ages – by the Tsars, by hermits, as rock cloisters…

In UNESCO's List of the World Cultural and Natural Heritage Sites Bulgaria has so far included: the Thracian Tomb near the town of Kazanlak; the Thracian Tomb near the village of Sveshtari; the hewn in living rock above an ancient heathen shrine Madara Horseman; Boyana Church near Sofia; Rila Monastery; the Rock Cloister near the village of Ivanovo not far from the Danube city of Rousse; the old part of the town of Nesebar on the southern Black Sea coast; the managed wetland reserve 'Srebarna' by the Lower Danube some 20 km west of the town of Silistra; and Pirin Mountain National Park. This, however, is apparently quite little in view of what this land has to offer. There is a proposal to add to the List the Thracian temples and vaults recently discovered near the villages of Starosel and Alexandrovo, the whole of the historical and archaeological reserve 'Sboryanovo' located on the area occupied in the distant past by the ancient Dausdava, the capital of the Thracians-Geti, the largest megalith in Europe – Perperikon - with the palace-shrine of the Thracian Tsars, the Christian temple 'Sveti 40 machenitsi' (the Holy 40 Martyrs) in the city of Veliko Tarnovo, the bone-vault in Bachkovo Monastery and the Old Town on one of the hills of the city of Plovdiv.

More than 1500 stone votive tablets with the image of the Thracian Horseman, Heros, have been found in Bulgaria, some of them being even built in churchs' altars or votive places. However, the Horseman is not only a relic of the antique past. The Horseman stands on icons and on the most prominent places in the Christian temples in the lands of ancient Thracians. Indeed, since 865 AD when Christianity was adopted as the official religion of the state, Bulgarian iconographers have painted him with the images of the saints-horsemen Georgi Pobedonosets (George the Victor) and Dimitar Solunski. Though they hold very much in reverence the days of St. George and St. Dimitar, the descendants of the ancient Thracians celebrate Heros in another day. It is not a fixed date of the calendar as it follows the ancient mystical moon calendar and the masquerade mysteries of the Koukers. The day is called Toudorovden (the Day of Toudor) and is celebrated with horse races called 'koushii'. Heros was the immortal demon (spirit) of a dear diseased, who stayed between the earthly and unearthly worlds ready to come to the aid of his living relatives. Though complemented with Christian symbolism, the feast actually is a celebration of the ancestors-protectors and during these 'koushii' (horse races) the living ones run the race in honour of 'the diseased ones' with horses adorned with bunches of hellebore and wild geranium. The winner gets a garland (the Dionysus garland!) and all people accompany him to his home. There a young girl welcomes him and offers him to drink a mixture of wine and water from little white (tinned) copper – exactly as depicted in the scenes on frescoes in the in-mound temples bequeathed us by the ancient Thracians!

And every even year in the city of Pernik (member of the Federation of European carnival cities) about 90 koukers', jamal's and sourvakars' groups with at least 3500 participants from all over the country perform their conjuring-fertilising mysteries during the international festival of the masquerade games. The feast is held by the end of January or the beginning of February, in the open on the central square of the town and on top of all else it is a competition. And neither the snowfall, nor the temperatures below the zero (quite frequently -10^0C or even -15^0C) can diminish the enthusiasm of both participants and the international jury, and the audience.

All of them are warmed not only by the delight of the sight but also by all stamping their feet in the rhythm of the kettle-drum, the squeal of pipes, the song of the copper bells hanging from the koukers' sashes, and the singing while they dance.

The mystical rites of the ancient Thracians keep on living in people's feasts of their descendants, Bulgarians of the present day. Every guests of our country can see that not only in villages and at the places of ancient shrines but even in big cities many Bulgarians perform the Thracians Dionysus' mysteries with the Koleda (Christmas) processions in the beginning of the year; with the koukers' festivals (when - hidden behind terrible ancient masks - the men chase away the evil from their land); with the 'Tsars of the vineyards' elected for the Day of Trifon Zarezan by their wine intoxicated suites; with the magical fires the young men leap across on Annunciation; with the nestinarki enraptured by divine ecstasy who dance barefooted on live embers (this dance can be seen every summer in the ancient ritual dance performed by dancers at many places on the southern Black Sea coast); with healing wonder-working and charms made in the shortest night of the year – that of June 24th, Enyovden (the Midsummer Day, or the birthday of St. John the Baptist)…

Even the Muslims dwelling in these lands for only several centuries have obeyed the Dionysus' Bacchic mysteries and the mysteries of the Holy Rock. This in fact is the reason why by many of the old shrines of the Thracians the Muslims have erected their own temples, but the wonder-workings they perform at sites like Demir Baba Teke (which was built upon the remains of a heathen shrine near the ancient Dausdava), by Perperek and at other similar places are far from being looked condescendingly at by the orthodox Islam…

Many of these manifestations of the traditional people's culture in the ways the rites are performed in different parts of the country can be seen together at the numerous special people's gatherings and singing competitions, as those held every year in the place called Predela in the region of Blagoevgrad, at the summit Rozhen in the Rodopi Mountains, in the southern Rodopi town of Zlatograd, region of Kardzhali or either at the national fair of folk songs and dances in the Sredna Gora town of Koprivshtitsa (which every fifth year becomes an international event). On such a fair where folk singers had gathered, many years ago the song 'Izlel e Delyo haydoutin' (Delyo – a male first name – the freedom fighter has come out) was recorded and the record put on a gold disk was sent with the space ship 'Voyager' in the deep of space to tell, as the case may be, to the possible extraterrestrial rational beings about the wondrous cosmic world of the man of the Earth. Bulgarian folk songs have been heard for a long time in non-Bulgarian movies (like the Canadian 'Jesus of Montreal' or from the reels of Emir Kostouritsa), in performances of world famous stars like Peter Gabriel, at the concerts of Goran Bregovich and the 'Mystery of Bulgarian voices'…

The songs in the sacred mountain of Orpheus are still working wonders, says the Japanese Prof. Kamioka. He's been here for ten or so times, arriving from Tokyo to collect melodies from the village of Davidkovo in the Rodopi Mountains. The Japanese team that visits Bulgaria together with him has recorded more than 200 Rodopi folk songs in the authentic performance of the village residents. Along with writing down the unusual melodies in notes Prof. Kamioka studies also the therapeutic effect of the mountain music. According to him, the slow, melodious Rodopi folk songs possess healing power but he is still studying whether the music exerts its positive effect outside the magnificent natural environment. If the presence of the latter proves to be a binding condition, the villagers are ready to welcome Japanese tourists who would come on the spot to be subjected to the healing powers of the songs from Orpheus' mountain.

Travellers too, will discover from now on the favourable influence the natural environment here exercises.

The ancients used to declare that nowhere in the world are there so many wonderful medicinal herbs and that people living here have been able for millennia to prepare magic extracts. Endless seems to the eye the diversity of curative places related with natural phenomena and unique reserves of the biosphere. The curing properties of more than 800 warm mineral springs, around which life is bustling from the dawn of civilisation and where renowned balneo-therapy centres have been set up for a very long time have undergone the examination of at least 8000 years of testing and 'clinical' trials.

This is a land that has always said welcome and farewell to travellers. Though all possible ethnic groups co-exist on it there are no ethnic conflicts between them. Here the guest is held in esteem; people of other faiths are respected; efforts are put to please the stranger. This is the reason for the increasing number of people from abroad coming here not only to have a nice holiday on the Black Sea coast. Although along its Bulgarian part the seashore offers the most tender sand, the most divers hotel complexes and the unforgettable south-European menu with dishes prepared from ecologically clean products more and more people arrive here in search for richer and more divers experiences. Apart from the huge streams of holiday-makers that have come to bathe in the sun on the beaches or 'museum' tourists, every year more than 150,000 people visit the country only to watch the migrating or breeding birds at Bourgas lakes, around the lake-reserve of Srebarna by the Danube, in the vicinity of the town of Madzharovo in the Eastern Rodopi Mountains and in many other places.

Conditions for the green and rural tourism are constantly improving and an increasing number of guests look for unforgettable experiences the living among authentic natural surroundings and people from all types of ethnic groups could give them when they share their everyday way of living, their cuisine, the wisdom of their ancient cultural principles. And there are entire villages in Bulgaria with their authentic 19th century architecture very well preserved like Bozhentsi, Zheravna, Dolen, Kovachevitsa to mention a few – a special present for the connoisseurs.

Traditional for the country are the rich hunting grounds: hunting was royal test for the ancient Thracians, a real passion for the Slavs and entertainment for Goths, elite pursuit for the old Bulgarians. This is the reason to have more and more hunters from abroad arriving here to enjoy the fascination of being among connoisseurs, while the trophies they acquire become the pride of their collections. There are trophies from red deer that have achieved 4 times the world records and the animals were shot in Bulgarian hunting grounds; trophies from boars and wild cats have also achieved world records for Bulgaria.

For mountain hikers there are exceptionally interesting routes in so different by their nature Bulgarian mountains: the 'alpine' type Rila and Pirin, the intimate and populated like the Rodopi,

Strandja and Sredna Gora… One of these mountains, Stara Planina or the Balkan Mountains (that gave its name to the entire peninsula) divides the country from its western border to the Black Sea in the east and along its main ridge goes the European Mountain Hikers' Route E-3. Along the ridges of some other of the Bulgarian mountains, Rila and Pirin, goes another European Mountain Hikers' Route, E-4 – from the Pyrenees to Peloponnesus. The mountaineers can find in Bulgaria excellent cliffs to climb, while more than 4700 caves wait invitingly the cave explorers. Some of the finest ones like Magourata, Ledenika, Saeva Doupka in Stara Planina Mountains or the Fore-Balkan, the Dyavolskoto Garlo (Devil's Throat), Yagodinskata Peshtera, Snezhanka in the Rodopi Mountains are lighted up and adapted for tourists' visits. Many of the above caves were inhabited in the antiquity. The most renowned among them is Magourata in Northwest Bulgaria: the so far discovered galleries have a total length of about 2500 m, some of the halls are more than 200 m long, more than 50 m wide and more than 20 m high-and the most curious thing about it – there one can see samples of the most interesting masterpieces of primitive art in the Balkans in more than 100 drawings from the early Bronze Age…

Bulgaria is the perfect place for you to create your own history with exciting memories from the life of all ages of the European civilisation, with the conveniences offered by the magnificent modern hotels and holiday villages. Along with the seaside resort complexes that many of the guests to the country have grown fond of, the attraction of high-mountain resorts with their superb conditions for winter sports is becoming increasingly powerful. Places that offer the tourist most pleasant pastime, recreation and entertainment are the town of Bansko in Pirin Mountain, the resort Borovets in Rila Mountain and Pamporovo in the Rodopi Mountains but for busy people the higher parts of Vitosha can be reached in a 30 to 40 minutes ride from Sofia.
Apart from health, energy and good comlpexion, holiday in Bulgaria will give you the chance to acquire original works of Bulgarian artists, heirs of the oldest painters in Europe. Authentic works of the traditional Bulgarian crafts can be bought from many ethnographic studios where you can watch how the artisans work out their wonderful masterpieces.

It is not easy to get everything in such a little book about a country like Bulgaria. But along the roads that expect you here you will feel what attracts you most powerfully among this astonishing diversity. Then you will have only to look for the publishing house that has made you this little gift and to present yourself with a bigger one from the rich collection it offers you.
We believe that our best meetings are yet to come and we are happy that we will see each other as good old friends!

1. Veliko Tarnovo, the hill of Tsarevets and the Patriarchal church: a general view

2. Spacious flattened ridges in Vratsa's divide of Stara Planina Mountains above the mountain chalet of Parshevitsa. The snow cover lasting from December until April and the availability of 4 ski-tows offer excellent opportunities for winter sports

3. Lakatnik cliffs: the most picturesque part of the Iskar Gorge. Rising to a height of up to 320 m above the river Iskar, with its 15 blazed alpine tracks of varying degree of difficulty and about 30 caves, the longest of which - the Temnata Doupka cave - exceeds 6 km in length are indeed heavenly corners for mountaineers and cave explorers (speleologists). Declared as a protected natural site with a surface area of 93 ha.

4. A general view of the village of Zgorigrad and Vratsa's divide of Stara Planina Mountains

5. The resort complex 'Slanchev Bryag' (Sunny Beach)
6. Bansko: one of the biggest winter resort complexes in Bulgaria: a general view
7. The reserve of architecture 'Bozhentsi' in winter
8. Smolyan, one of the prettiest towns in Bulgaria, picturesquely set in the valley of river Cherna in Rodopi Mountains
9. Nesebar: the old town, a reserve of architecture and history located on a small peninsula on the Black Sea coast; today is on UNESCO's List of the World Cultural and Natural Heritage Sites

10. Sofia: a general view out on the south districts
of the city with Vitosha Mountain in the background

11. Sofia: Banski Square

12. The Monument of the Unknown Soldier in front of the south wall of the ancient church of 'Sveta Sofia'. The monument is a tomb with a sarcophagus and 5 stone urns containing the bones of soldiers that died for Bulgaria as well as soil from all four corners of the country. A low tombstone is placed on pavement made of granite blocks, surrounded by a balustrade. In a round bronze sacrificial altar resting on 4 swords an eternal flame burns, while to the left there is a recumbent lion sculptured by the artist Prof. Andrey Nikolov some 80 years ago. On a massive stone slab decorated with two bronze crowns of laurel the following lines from a poem by the famous Bulgarian poet Ivan Vazov have been engraved:

'Bulgaria, they died for you
you - one and only - was worthy to them
and they were worthy to you'

13. More than 100 burial mounds (hillocks) of

diameter up to 45 m and height up to 9 m situated singly or grouped in up to 8 together could be seen in Sofia proper or in the city's outskirts. Here is shown a burial mound in Sofia district of Orlandovtsi

14. Remains of a bathhouse, part of the late-antique Serdica (4th century AD), supplied with water from a piped hot mineral spring, preserved till present day in the basement of the Central Shopping Mall (Central Hali)

15. The Eastern Gate of ancient Serdica, 4th century AD

16. The Western Gate of ancient Serdica: stone blocks with inscriptions

13

14

15   16

43

17

18

17. Sarcophagi from a mausoleum in Sofia's South Park, 4th century AD
18. A street in ancient Serdica that ran by the imperial complex of Constantine the Great

19

19. Remains of a late-antiquity public building near the church 'Sveti Georgi' (Saint George)
20. The Doctor's Garden: a corner where antique inscriptions, tombstones, sarcophagi, columns and architectural details from ancient buildings in Sofia are shown

20

22

23

21

24

21. The Museum of Archaeology: accommodated in a building erected in the period 1451 through 1453 and known as the 'Byuuk Jamiya' (The Big Mosque)

22 - 24. The church 'Sveti Georgi' (Saint George the Victor) known as the Rotunda: the best preserved antique architectural monument within the limits of Sofia. It is part of a building the function of which is not fully clear to experts, erected by the end of the 4th century AD at the time of Emperor Constantine the Great and since 10th century reconstructed as a Christian temple. Five layers of wall paintings dated between 10th and 16th centuriy, of exceptional artistic value, are still preserved. Since 1989 the church has been declared a museum and since 1998 it has been restored its function as a patron-temple of the Bulgarian army

25

25 - 29. The temple-monument 'Sveti Alexander Nevski' erected in honour of those that fell for the Liberation of Bulgaria, later enunciated as a Patriarchal cathedral. Regarding its architecture the temple pertains to Byzantine cross-domed basilicas and has a length of 73.5 m, width of 55 m and height of 52 m. In the temple's bell-tower 12 bells cast in Tula and Moscow were mounted, the biggest one having a diameter of 3 m and weight of 11.7 tonnes. High above the main entrance,

26

immediately below the bell-tower, a mosaic portrait of Sveti Alexander Nevski stands out. It was made after the design of Bulgarian artist Anton Mitov. The church can hold up to 5000 churchgoers.

27

30. Since 1965 the crypt of the temple-monument "Sveti Alexander Nevski' has been turned into an art gallery, affiliated with the National Gallery of Fine Arts. Icons, wall paintings, church plates and sacred vessels, stamps and manuscripts from 4th till 19th century are exhibited there - unique specimens of the Old-Bulgarian and Renaissance art.

28

29

30

31

31 - 34. Sofia is a unique city: it is the only one in Europe that has not moved its administrative centre: preserved foundations of the complex from where in the beginning of the 4th century Constantine the Great gave his ordinances, and after him other Byzantine and Bulgarian bays-wearers, today are surrounded by the President's Palace. Where once Friedrich Barbarossa, Gotfried of Boulogne, Earl Robert of Flanders, Duke Robert of Normandy and Earl Raymond of Toulouse had stepped up with respect today their countries' heads of state pass during their official visits to Bulgaria.

32. The Council of Ministers' Building

33. The building of the National Assembly, 1886.

34. At the site where today the NATO's Alley has been formed, between the President's Palace and the building of the Council of Ministers, soon other parts of the ancient centre of the city will be revealed and exhibited to relate the story of the many millennia of life at that particular place

32

33

34

49

35

36

37

38

39

40

35 - 40. The aspect of Sofia changes constantly: by the numerous old buildings declared as monuments of culture rise new successful architectural solutions

41. National Palace of Culture. At the competition 'The best congress centre' organised by the International Association of the Congress Centres it ranked the second best congress centre in the world for the year 2003

42. National Theatre 'Ivan Vazov'. Built in 1907 after the design of the architects Helmer and Felner of Vienna. In a fire that burst out in 1923 the building was nearly destroyed and was restored in its today's appearance after the design of Prof. Dulfer of Dresden

41

42

43

44

45

46

43 - 46. Part of the memory of Sofia.

43. The monument of the Tsar-Liberator, 1907: the most impressive sculptural monument in Sofia, the work of the Florentine Arnoldo Dzocchi.

44. The monument of Stefan Stambolov, an eminent Bulgarian politician and scholar, Prime Minister of Bulgaria 1887-1894, assassinated in 1895.

45. The Doctors' Monument, erected in 1883 in memory of the medical military staff, doctors and medical orderlies that perished in the Russian-Turkish Liberation War 1877-1878.

46. The monument of Vasil Levski - the ideologist of the Bulgarian national revolution and founder of the Internal Revolutionary Organisation - erected on the spot where he was hanged by the Turkish authorities on February 19, 1873

47

47. "Sveta Sofia' (Saint Sofia): symbol of the capital city, a monumental sculpture of the artist Georgi Chapkanov

48. Bulbank and the church 'Sveta Petka Samardjiyska'

49. Plastic work by the sculptor Georgi Chapkanov in front of the National Theatre 'Ivan Vazov'

50. Station 'Serdica' of the underground railway in front of Bulbank

48

49

50

51

53

51 - 52. The Central Department Store (TsUM) the biggest shopping mall in the capital city

53. The art composition 'Nest', a work by Georgi Chapkanov, in front of the church 'Sveti Sedmochisle-nitsi' (The Seven Saints)

54. A piece of plastic art by Georgi Chapkanov in the small garden near the Central Hali (the old central shopping mall)

52   54

55

56

55 - 56. The Central Hali:
the covered shopping mall of
Sofia. The building designed
in the style secession was
erected in 1909; above its
main entrance Sofia's coat of
arms was built in along with
its motto: 'Ever growing,
never ageing' and above it, a
fretwork clock tower.

57. Vitosha Boulevard:
a multi-storeyed street
silhouette with scores of
modern boutiques

59

58 - 59. Centre for folk arts and crafts: more than 3600 kinds of traditional Bulgarian souvenirs are offered to customers in the Centre's shops located in the National Museum of Ethnography and not far from the church 'Sveta Sofia'. The souvenirs are handmade after authentic technologies, from natural raw materials; most of them are also exact copies of museum exhibits

60. 'Knigomania' – the biggest chain of bookshops for foreign literature; offers over 20 000 titles in Russian and English but also Bulgarian ones

60

62. Slaveykovs' Square: a unique open-air book market, open the year round, without a day off

63. An art composition by Georgi Chapkanov in the small garden by the Central Hali (the old central shopping mall)

64. Under today's hotel 'Rila' are the remains of the south-east tower of the fortified wall of ancient Serdica

61

62

63   64

65

67

66

68

65 - 66. Amusement park
'Sofia land'. Twenty-three
attractions - among them a
34-m high Ferris wheel - offer
exclusive excitements and
entertainment

67. 'Orlov Most' (The
Eagle Bridge): a detail of its
monumental ornamentation

69 - 75. Vitosha, one of the most beautiful and popular Bulgarian mountains, raises its massive dome very close to the south of Sofia. Stone rivers (moraines); plateau-like areas arranged in storeys with the highest summit above them all, the Cherni Vrah, at 2290 m asl; expansive peat bogs, from which clear and fast-flowing rivers take their beginning; ages old spruce forests; astonishing biodiversity: more than 2700 species of vascular plants only; karst springs; the longest cave in Bulgaria (Doukhlata, 16.5 km) - these are a part only

69

of the landmarks for which
the mountain was declared as
early as in 1934 a national park
The snow cover on Vitosha,
quite good for winter sports,
lasts between 4 and 6 months;
the well-developed network
of lifts, towlines, ski runs of
altitude ranging between 1650
and 2290 m asl, more than 270
km blazed mountain tracks,
4 centres of curative mineral
springs, 10 monasteries, more
than 15 hotels as well as its
closeness to Sofia make this
mountain a wonderful place
for recreation and
entertainment

72

74

73   75

76 - 83. Boyana church is located in Sofia's district of Boyana, on one of the northern slopes of Vitosha Mountain and is rated among one of the most significant monuments of the Bulgarian Middle Ages, entered UNESCO's List of the World Cultural and Natural Heritage Sites. Its wall paintings dated from two periods: 11th-12th and 13th-14th century mark a summit in the achievements of the Tarnovo school of art and have been defined as one of the most valuable Bulgarian contributions to the medieval European painting

76

77   78

79   80

81

82

83

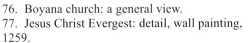

76. Boyana church: a general view.

77. Jesus Christ Evergest: detail, wall painting, 1259.

78. Life of Sveti Nikola (St. Nicolas): The miracle at the sea, wall painting, 1259;

79. Life of Sveti Nikola: The three strategs thank Sveti Nikola: detail, wall painting, 1259;

80. The descent into hell: detail, wall painting, 1259;

81. Christ among the scribes, wall painting, 1259.

82. Sebastocrator Kaloyan and sebastocratoress Desislava, portrait of the donors, wall painting, 1259;

83. Tsar Constantine-Assen the Quiet and Tsarina Irina, wall painting, 1259.

84 - 90. The Sofia Mala Sveta Gora (i.e. the Little Holy Mount): a centre of more than 90 monasteries in the countryside around today's Sofia, the majority of which were established as early as in 9th - 14th century; in Malomalovski Monastery 'Sveti Nikolay Mirlikiyski' (St. Nikolas from the town of Mir in Lykia, Asia Minor); murals from the 16th century in Kremikovtsi Monastery 'Svety Georgi' (St. George the Victor), preserved murals in the church of 1493 of the Nedelishte Monastery 'Sveti Anastasiy Aleksandriyski' (St Anastasios of Alexandria), 16th

84

86   85

87   88

century, a general view; pieces of stone plastic arts and fantastic facemask - a combination of human face and an animal head, painted on the right side of the altar, in breach of the church canon; Dragalevtsi Monastery 'Sveta Bogoroditsa' (The Holy Mother), founded in 1345 by Tsar Ivan-Alexander – well-preserved mural decorations from 1476; Seslavtsi Monastery 'Sveti Nikolay Mirlikiyski (see above): mural decorations from 1616.

91. A river Vit gorge at the village of Sadovets, region of Pleven

92

93

94

92 - 100. The bridges - a means for communi-
cating with other people
92. A bridge over the river Maritsa in the town of
Svilengrad: 300-m long, 6-m wide with 20 vaults.
A plate with an inscription reads that the bridge was
built in 1529 during the rule of Mustafa Pasha 'as a
good deed'.
93 - 94. A bridge over river Yantra close to the town
of Byala, region of Rousse. Work of the master-
builder Nikola Fichev; it is 276 m long, 9 m wide,
with 14 vaults, decorated with exquisite stone pieces
of plastic arts, completed 1865.
95. The bridge with lions near the town of Apriltsi
96. A bridge in the Rodopi Mountains town of
Madan
97. A bridge over the river Strouma (with 5 vaults)
by the village of Nevestino, region of Kyustendil:
an inscription in Turkish language testifies that

95

96   97

98   99

the bridge was built in 1469 during the reign of Sultan Mohamed II

98 - 99. The Devil's bridge on river Arda, near the village of Dyadovtsi, region of Kardjali. The bridge is 56 m long, 3.5 m wide and on one of the key-stones there is the sign of a hexagon.

100. A modern bridge over river Bebresh on 'Hemus' highway; this is the highest bridge in Bulgaria

100

101. Plovdiv: the second biggest and most important city in Bulgaria located picturesquely on the two banks of river Maritsa on 6 syenite hills (the so-called 'tepe')

102 - 103. Plovdiv: a general view out to the centre of the city

104 - 105. The antique theatre, 2nd century AD: a general view

103   104

105

106   107

108

107. A renaissance house in the Old Plovdiv

108. Part of the antique forum, 2nd century AD: the largest ensemble of this type discovered so far in ancient Thrace

109. An antique stadium (2nd century AD): the northern sector, the so-called sphendon and Jumma mosque - one of the oldest Ottoman cult buildings

109

in the Balkan Peninsula, erected during the reign of Sultan Mourad II in mid-15th century

110. The Roman-Catholic cathedral 'Sveti Ludwig' (St. Louis), erected in 1861 after the design of the Rome architect Alfonso

111 - 113. Architectural ensembles in Plovdiv. A house belonging to Dimitar Georgiadi: the facade with the main entrance, 1848 /bottom, right/

110

111

112   113

114   115

116   117

114. Bachkovo Monastery 'The Assumption': the second largest after the Rila Monastery and one of the oldest in Bulgaria. Established in 1083 by the Georgian Grigory Bakouriani, Sebast (a governor) and Grand Domestic of the Byzantine army

115. The church-ossuary at the Bachkovo Monastery. Located some 300 to 400 m east of the present-day monastery, also erected in 1083. The steeply sloped ground had been skilfully used for differentiating two storeys: a lower one adapted as a chapel with a vault and the upper one, as the church proper. In the church, there are preserved murals dated 11th century

AD, worked by the Georgian artist Iberopoulets as well as the donor's portrait of Tsar Ivan-Alexander painted in 14th century

116. After destroying the monastery by fire, by the end of 16th century restorations works were commenced and on the foundations of the old church the new cathedral temple 'The Assumption' was erected

117. In 1643 the south wing of the monastery was built along with the refectory, which was also richly decorated with religious paintings. 'The antique philosophers' and the 'Doomsday': murals in the monastery's refectory

118

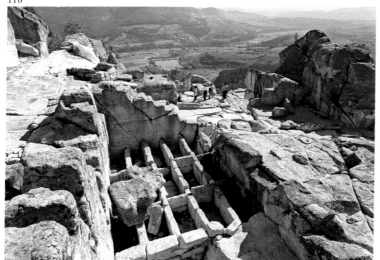

119

118 - 120. The mountain top where spirits abide: this is what the local people call a rocky summit rising high above the surrounding area near the village of Gorna Krepost, region of Kardjali. And else Perpericon is the name of the most unbelievable complex revealed in recent years during archaeological excavations at the same hill. The rock massif had been worshipped since the Neolithic times, i.e. the end of 6th - the beginning of the 5th millennium BC and had been in use without interruption for different purposes until the 14th century AD: a sanctuary, which had grown into a grandiose cult centre and later into an antique and medieval town. According to ancient written traditions here, in this temple, the world history had been twice pre-designed. The first time it was Alexander the Great to whom the oracle said that he would conquer the world, and then - in the 1st century BC the father of Octavianus Augustus became aware that his son would established the Roman Empire upon the ruins of the Republic.

120

121. Mechi kladenets (the bear's well): the most ancient copper mine in Europe, dated back to the 4th millennium BC. Located near the city of Stara Zagora and consisting of 6 mining developments that has been traced out to a depth of 18 m. During the excavations carried out there archaeologists found numerous fragments of ceramics and mining 'tools' as well as remains of the miners' ancient dwellings. It has been estimated that some 1000 tonnes of copper were produced from this mine alone and distributed as far away as the land of today's Ukraine. In the famous Karbouna treasure only, the number of copper articles made of the metal produced at Mechi Kladenets, exceeds 400.

122. Thracian rock vault by the village of Tatoul, region of Kardjali, 1st millennium BC

123. Rock niches not far from the village of Ardino, region of Kardjali, most likely used for some cult purposes, 1st millennium BC

124. The dolmens are the oldest monuments of the monumental tomb architecture in Bulgarian land, 1st millennium BC

125. Rock drawings in the cave Magourata, near the village of Rabisha, region of Vidin, 3rd - 2nd millennium BC

126. Thracian shrine in a cave near the village of Baylovo, region of Sofia

122

123   124

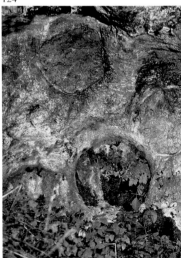

125   126

127 - 128. Thracian cult complex Starosel. So far 6 temples have been discovered under mounds; of these 4 are unique.

Chetinyova mogila: a general view. It is fenced off with a wall (called 'krepida') made of cut stones and having a length of 241 m and a height of about 3.5 m. The biggest Thracian temple found in Bul-garian land was discovered un-der this knoll. The temple con-sists of a 10-m long and 6-m wide corridor and two premi-ses: a rectangular one and a round one, the diameter of the

127

128

129

130

131

132

latter being 5.4 m and its height, 6 m. Dated 5th century BC.

129 - 130. Ruins of the temple found under the knoll 'Horizont' (Horizon): as of today the only known temple with a colonnade in Thrace - 10 round columns, standing on column bases and with capitals in early Doric style, 4th century BC.

131. Thracian domed vault by the village of Mezek, district of Svilengrad, 4th century BC

132. Thracian shrine near the village of Kasnakovo, region of Haskovo: the central spring. Includes cult buildings (2nd century), an inn (3rd century), an amphitheatre (4th century) and an architectural design of the three springs that has them arranged in a half-ellipse. An ancient-Greek inscription there reads: "Well met! Titus Flavius Beytyukent Esbenerios and his wife Claudia Montana built and dedicated this spring to the nymphs and Aphrodite."

133

133. Thracian domed vault near the town of
Kazanlak, 4th century BC. Mural ornamentation in
the funeral chamber of the vault is of exceptional
artistic value. The vault by Kazanlak has been
entered UNESCO's List of the World Cultural and
Natural Heritage Sites

134 - 137. City of Haskovo: a regional centre and
a university town, which celebrated its 1000th
anniversary in 1985. Not far from Haskovo, by
the village of Klokotnitsa on March 9, 1230 the
fateful for Bulgaria battle took place, in which Tsar
Ivan-Assen II (1218-1241) defeated the Byzantine
who had treacherously violated a signed peace
treaty and captured the despot of Epirus, Theodor I
Komnin. After that battle Bulgaria again bordered

on three seas: the Black Sea in the east, the Aegean in the south, and the Adriatic in the west. Over the city rises the monument of the Holy Mother of God; it stands 31.40 m high and is the tallest sculptural effigy of Virgin Mary in the world

134   135

136   137

138 - 141. Zlatograd is the southernmost Bulgarian town of a 500-year history. Its picturesque natural surroundings are noteworthy by their exceptional biological and particularly botanical diversity; the climate in this region is mild and is influenced tangibly by the Mediterranean; there are hot mineral springs, well-preserved monuments of architecture and renaissance traditions, crafts and customs. If a man lands there he will enjoy an unforgettable pastime and will long for returning again and again in this heavenly corner of Bulgaria.

138

139

140   141

142 - 145. Zlatograd sings and dances… Every year amateur companies for folklore songs and dances meet in Zlatograd at the national fair-and-singing competition 'The Rodopi Mountains and the Space'. Zlatograd is the birthplace of the famous folk song 'Izlel e Delyo Haydoutin' (Delyo the Haydout has come out to fight the oppressors of his people). Sung by the renowned Rodopi Mountains folklore singer Valya Balkanska and recorded on a gilded disk together with 26 other songs from all over the world the song was sent in 1977 in the deep space on the spaceship 'Voyager' as a poetic message to the future…

The place where the Zlatograd-born Delyo Voyvoda was killed.

The monument of Delyo Voyvoda in the town's centre.

Participants in the annual fair.

The church 'Sveti Georgi Pobedonosets' (St George the Victor) and part of the founded in 1852 reciprocal school

1

147   148

146 - 149. Bansko: a re-
naissance charm and magnificent nature. Narrow mean-
dering cobbled streets,
two-storey fortified houses
built of stone and wood and
fenced with tall stone walls
with heavy wooden gates,
their facades decorated with
murals, shadowed verandas
and unique architecture -
one can see all this and
much more in one of the
newest winter resorts in
Bulgaria on the background
of the Pirin Mountain's
majestic silhouette

149

150 - 152. Bansko: more than 150 of its houses have been declared monuments of architecture.
The town square is dominated by the 30-m tall bell-tower with a clock, and the powerful stone bulk of the church 'Sveta Troitsa' (The Holy Trinity), a three-nave pseudo-basilica, the second biggest in Bulgaria after the temple-monument 'Sveti Alexander Nevski' in Sofia.
40 private hotels and more than 100 cosy catering establishments with sumptuous Bulgarian cuisine and places for entertainment are at the disposal of the tourist in Bansko

150

151   152

85

153

154

153 - 157. Bansko actually is an all-season resort and the point of departure for outings in the Pirin Mountain of which 40,332 ha constitute the second biggest national park in Bulgaria, entered UNESCO's List of the World Cultural and Natural Heritage Sites.
176 lakes are known for the Pirin Mountain, the biggest of all being the 'Popovo ezero' (lake) with a surface area of 12.4 ha. Among the most frequently visited lakes are those located in the Banderitsa cirque, above the mountain chalet of Vihren

155

156   157

158   159

158 - 161. Ski-centre 'Bansko' with the highest point at an altitude of 2560 m asl, the lowest one at 1000 m asl, total length of blazed ski runs of 56 km, total length of the chair- and gondola lifts of 16 km and of the ski-tows, 6 km. There is also equipment for making artificial snow, 12 snow-ramming machines, and a life-saving service on a round-the-clock duty: this is only a part of the of the resort's technical characteristics

160

161

162. Ski run "Alberto Tomba"

163. General view of Bansko
from the 4-seat lift leading
to Banderitsa plateau and the
summit Todorka. Vis-à-vis
are the snow-capped peaks
of Rila Mountain with the
highest peak in the Balkan
Peninsula, the Moussalla,
(2925 m asl)

164. The site Banderishka
Polyana at 1635 m asl is the
gondola lift upper station and
is always busy with people

162

163   164

165. Melnik, the smallest town in Bulgaria, located at the southern feet of Pirin Mountain at 200 m asl. Declared a reserve of architecture and a museum town, with more than 100 of its houses rising in tiers upon tiers on the steep slopes of picturesque sandstone rocks are registered as monuments of culture. Another sight in the town is its wine cellars, dug in the soft sandstone and numbering over 70. The famous Melnik wine, which in the past was exported to as far as Vienna, Genoa and Venice, seasons in them

16?

166   167

168

169

166. The 'Byzantine house',
14th century, in Melnik
167. Melnik houses
168. A corner of the town

169. Some of the Melnik
pyramids rise as high as 100
m above the ground. They
cover an area of 8.5 ha and
have been declared a natural
landmark

170. Rozhen Monastery
'The Birth of the Mother of
God'. Founded in 1220 but
has acquired its contemporary
appearance by the end of 18th
century

170

171. Waterfall Polska Skakavitsa in the Zemen Gorge of river Strouma

172 - 173. Galabin rocks: one of the numerous bizarre looking rock groups in the Zemen Gorge of river Strouma

171   172

173

174 - 177. The Zemen Monastery: a medieval monastery located on the left bank of river Strouma in the Zemen Gorge. The church was erected in 9th century and preserves murals from 11th and 14th centuries. By their style and iconographic peculiarities the murals from the 14th century differ from the officially adopted medieval painting canons and are closer to the old, archaic art schools making them one of the most intriguing monuments of Bulgarian monumental art of that time

174

175   176

177

178 - 187. Koukers' games are in fact a folklore theatre art expressing by the means of mimics, dances, costumes and masks, occasionally by a dialogue, certain ideas and rites of symbolic-magic meaning, blessings for good health, fertility and prosperity. They contain some elements of pre-historic pagan traditions whose roots are lost in the depths of time but today are inestimable cultural wealth that has preserved until present day the spiritual make-up and national identity of Bulgarians.

Every even year an International Festival of Masquerade Games is held in the city of Pernik where one can trace out the full riches and diversity of the characters, rites, and koukers' requisites and can feel the heightened emotionality of participants

179

180   181

182   183

184

185   186

188. The Mushroom: a natural landmark near the village of Beli Plast, region of Kardjali

189. Belogradchik rocks: a gigantean rock world that strikes imagination with wondrous shapes sculptured by the natural elements. More than 160 years ago the famous French traveller Jerome Blanki wrote: "Neither the renowned defiles at Ollioul in Provence, nor the Pancarbeaux in Spain, nor the Alps, the Pyrenees, nor the divine mountains of Tirol and Switzerland could be compared with what the eye sees in Bulgaria at Belogradchik"

188

189

190 - 193. The fountains of Samokov. Building of fountains is an ancient tradition preserved till present day. The fountains must be made of stone in order to last for centuries. They must be beautifully designed and built in order to bring joy… The decorated fountain… The fountain with the earring, 1662. Decorated with a little stone bird's nesting-box and an 'earring' consisting of three parts, carved out one into another of a single stone block

190

191

192   193

194

195   196

194 - 197. Borovets, the oldest winter resort in Bulgaria, is located at an altitude of 1350 m asl in the Moussalla divide of Eastern Rila Mountain and is the point of departure for a number of tracks both for crossing the whole of the mountain and for climbing to the highest peak in Bulgaria and in the Balkan Peninsula, Moussalla, rising to 2925 m asl. From Borovets one can come out to the Moussalla cirque where there are 7 pictu-resque mountain lakes. One of these, Ledenoto (the Icy) lake is located at the highest altitude in the Balkans, at 2709 m asl

197

198 - 201. There are three ski-centres at Borovets. They have 15 blazed ski runs of different classes of difficulty, and the special sound and lighting systems installed at some of them allow skiing at night, from 17.00 until 22.00 h. One gondola lift going up to the summit of Yastrebets (2369 m asl), two chair-lifts, 10 ski tows and 3 portable mini-tows with a total length of about 15 km are at the disposal of the numerous lovers of winter sports that visit the resort.
202. Rila: a general view from the summit of Yastrebets

198

199

200   201

203 - 209. Rila Monastery is the biggest and the most visited of the Bulgarian monasteries. It was founded in the 10th century and treasures invaluable documents and other material evidence on Bulgarian history and culture. on UNESCO's List of the World Cultural and Natural Heritage Sites

203

204

205

206

207

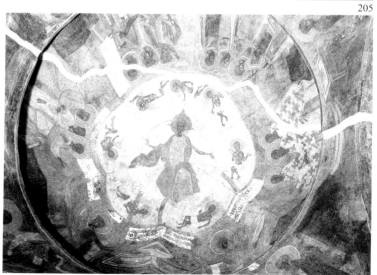

208

209

210 - 211. Koprivshtitsa: a reserve of architecture and history and a museum town, with more than 380 architectural and historical monuments. Fine houses built from stone and wood decorated with murals, alafrangas and ceilings made of carved wood, fairy inner yards with flower beds, cobbled paths, wells and stone fountains, narrow steep streets, fenced with tall stone walls on both sides ...

210

211

212 - 215. Every year in August the Days of Folklore are held in Koprivshtitsa, while once every 5 years a National Folklore Fair takes place there. At these fairs dance and song companies from all over the country get together in an exuberant pageant of music, songs, dances and folk costumes

212

213   214

215

216 - 226. House next to a
house, a wall next to a wall,
a roof over the next roof:
the houses from the time
of the Renaissance embody
the love of Bulgarian for the
beauty and the cosiness of
the home. The bay-windows,
the fretwork tracery on semi-
opened premises, the use
of colonnades or wooden
lattices and covers, the change
of building materials and
coloration, the generous use
of carved wood and mural
decorations demonstrate both
artistic talent and the taste and
preferences of their creators

216

217

218

219

220

221   222

223   224

225   226

111

227 - 230. City of Sliven: located at the southern feet of Sliven divide of Stara Planina Mountains. There are well-preserved houses of renaissance architecture and an interesting church, 'Sveta Sofia', a single-nave domed church, originally erected probably in 11th-13th century. Of certain interest is the natural park 'Sinite kamani' (the Blue Rocks) with its spacious forests, rock massifs with impressive cliffs, caves and many historical monuments the earliest of which as old as the 5th century BC

227

228   229

230

231

231 - 235. Yambol: a town of ancient history on the banks of river Tundzha. It was founded by Thracians in the 3rd century BC, its Thracian name was Kabile, and was the largest military camp in the Roman province of Thrace. The city minted bronze and silver coins, there was a shrine dedicated to Zeus; was destroyed by the Goths in 378 AD. Later the city was restored and in the Middle Ages was named Dianopolis. Not far from it is the 'Erkesiya" - a defensive facility 131 km long on the border with the Byzantine Empire

232. The temple "Sveti Nikolay Chudotvorets' (Saint Nikolas the Thaumaturge)

233. Eski Jamiya (the Old Mosque): Islamic cult building erected in 1385

234. Ruins of ancient Kabile

235. The 'Bezisten' - a covered market place (bazaar) built in 15th century AD

232

233

234

235

236. The Kroushouna travertine cascade: picturesque waterfalls, the biggest of which is 15 m high, scores of little ponds situated in tiers, outlined by fine sinter walls with overflowing water gushing forth from a nearby cave - this is how one of the 7 operating eco-tracks in Bulgaria looks. Facilities made of wood like foot bridges, bridge railings and stairs make walking along the track easy and the unbelievable nature of this wonderful corner

accessible to everyone who visits the countryside near the village of Kroushouna in the region of Lovech

237 - 240. Nicopolis ad Istrum (the Town of Victory) on the bank by the Danube: this was what the Roman Emperor Trajanus named the newly

founded town in honour
of his victories over the
Dacians in 102-106 AD. By
the end of the 2nd century
AD the town reached its
heyday. Many temples with
colonnades, broad streets
paved with flagstones,
modern water supply and
sewerage system, parts of
which are still preserved,
marble and bronze statues
of deities, emperors and
honoured citizens turned it
into one of the largest and
urbanised Roman towns in
Bulgarian lands of those
times

237

239

238   240

241

242   243

241 - 243. Tarnovo: a fortress and a city of Tsars,
the capital of the Second Bulgarian State. The
earliest settlement was dated 4300 BC and was
located in the countryside area named Kachitsa in
today's western section of the city, while traces
from ancient settlement on the hill of Tsarevets
were dated 4200 BC. In 5th century AD an early-
Byzantine town had grown on Tsarevets and
in 1185 the uprising of Bulgarians against the
Byzantine rule broke. The uprising brought the
liberation of Bulgaria, while the peace treaty
from 1187 marked the beginning of the period
of Tarnovo as the capital of the Bulgarian State,
which lasted 206 years, until the fall of Bulgaria
under the Ottoman rule. Today's city of Veliko
Tarnovo is probably the most picturesque town in
Bulgaria, a university and regional administration
centre where every single stone is a piece of

history. The fortress on the hill of Tsarevets is the most popular museum item in the country visited every year by more than 150,000 Bulgarian and foreign tourists

244. The Monument of Assenevtsi (the dynastic house of Assens): dedicated to Bulgarian Tsars Assen I, Petar, Kaloyan and Ivan-Assen II. These were the rulers during the reign of which Bulgarian medieval state with the capital city of Veliko Tarnovo reached its political, economical and cultural zenith

244

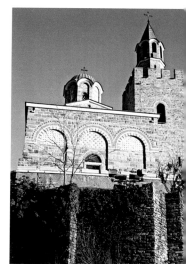

245

246   247

248

245. The Patriarchal cathedral on the hill of Tsarevets

246. The Patriarchal cathedral 'Vaznesenie Gospodne' (The Ascension of God): the interior

247. The Tower of Baldwin: it is assumed that in this tower Emperor Baldwin of Flanders was kept as a prisoner of war after he was captured in the battle at Odrin (today's Edirne in Turkey) in 1205 AD by the Bulgarian Tsar Kaloyan

248. The church 'Sveti Dimitar Solunski' (St. Dimitar of Salonika): here in 1185 the uprising led by Petar and Assen against the Byzantine rule was declared. This uprising brought Bulgaria its freedom and the restoration of the Bulgarian independent state.

249

250

252

249 - 252. The church 'Sveti Petar and Pavel (St. Peter and Paul), erected by the end of 13th century, today is one of the best preserved medieval churches in Veliko Tarnovo. After Bulgaria fell under Ottoman rule the Bulgarian Patriarchate and the patriarchal library were moved in this church. There are three layers of paintings from the 14th, 16th and 17th century - real masterpieces of Bulgarian medieval painting

251

253

254

253 - 258. Arbanasi: a village where architecture of the 15th-18th century is well preserved. Today it is a reserve of architecture, a museum and tourist centre. 143 buildings in it have been declared monuments of culture. The exterior and interior of the residential buildings show exceptional diversity; the decoration of individual premises has been brought to perfection, which is without a match in other parts of the country so there was every reason to set them apart in an architectural type of their own called 'the big Arbanasi house'. Of no less interest are the 7 Arbanasi churches built and wall-painted in several phases between 15th and 17th centuries. Their architectural, iconographic and style peculiarities as well as their preserved iconostases, icons, crosses made of carved wood, along with the church sacred plates and vessels and liturgical books have

such a great historical and artistic value that experts have deservedly defined them as a phenomenon of the Balkan culture and art of that period.

255

256

257

258

259   260

261

259 - 265. The Tarnovo Sveta Gora (Holy Mount): a centre of monasteries around the medieval Tarnovgrad (today's Veliko Tarnovo), erected around 10th – 14th century, put to fire and plundering many times and preserved in their renovated appearance till present day. The oldest among them is the Patriarchal Monastery 'Sveta Troitsa' (the Holy Trinity) /1/. It was the central literary school of Patriarch Evtimy Tarnovski. The other have emerged later, in 13th and 14th century supported by Bulgarian Tsars ("the great and pious Tsar Ivan-Assen founded monasteries and decorated them"; "Tsar Ivan-Alexander raised many monasteries and churches") and developed as educational centres for spiritual and cultural communion. Among these are the monasteries 'Sveti 40 machenitsi' (the Forty Holy Martyrs) /2/ near the village of Merdanya, founded in 1230; 'Sveto Preobrazhenie Gospodne' (the Holy Transfiguration of our Lord) /3/, the biggest of the monasteries around Veliko Tarnovo

and the forth biggest in Bulgaria, established in 1360; Kapinovo Monastery 'Sveti Nikola' /4, 5/ near the village of Kapinovo founded in 1272; 'Rozhdestvo Christovo' (the Birth of Christ) /6/ near the town of Kilifarevo, erected in 1348; and 'Sveti Ravnoapostoli Petar and Pavel' (the Saints Equal to the Apostles Peter and Paul) /7/ above the town of Lyaskovets, founded in 1185.

262

263

264   265

266

266 - 267. Pliska: the first
capital of the Bulgarian
State since it was established
until 893. Established as a
fortification, Pliska originally
was a residence of Bulgarian
princes and later developed
into a large medieval city
with three concentric rings of
fortified walls fencing in the
palace of the Bulgarian ruler

267

268 - 271. The reserve of history and archaeology 'Veliki Preslav'. Veliki Preslav is the second capital city of Bulgaria (from 893 until 972). Remains of the palace of Tsar Simeon. The round (golden) church in Preslav is a unique example of the old-Bulgarian architecture. Floor mosaic from Preslav

268   269

270   271

272. The Màdara Horseman: a rock bas-relief, hewn in living rock at the height of 23 m from the base of a big cliff near the village of Màdara, region of Shoumen, in the beginning of the 8th century. Depicts an almost life-size horseman piercing a lion with his spear; behind the horseman there is a running hound. There are several inscriptions in Greek around the image, which are a kind of chronicle about events that had taken place between 705 and 831 AD. The bas-relief proper symbolises the victories of Bulgarian rulers at the time of establishing the Bulgarian State in these lands. The Màdara Horseman is the only bas-relief hewn in living rock in the whole of Europe and was entered UNESCO's List of the World Cultural and Natural Heritage Sites.

273 - 275. At the feet of the cliffs where the Màdara Horseman was hewn archaeologists found traces of human

272

273

274

communal life dated as far
back as 3500 BC. During the
1st millennium BC in the Big
Cave under the cliffs, near a
big karst spring there was a
Thracian shrine of the three
nymphs-protectors of the
springs and givers of health.
During the late antiquity at
the foot of the cliffs a large
settlement gradually grew up
and in the early Middle Ages
Màdara was developed into
the most important cult centre
of the Bulgarian State before
the adoption of Christianity as
official religion. Later Màdara
had still preserved its role of
a cult centre: during 12th-14th
century more than 170 monk
cells and rock churches were
hewn in the cliffs, and on the
plateau above the cliffs stood
the Bulgarian fortress Màtora.
Today the area around Màdara
has the statute of reserve of
history and archaeology.

275

276 - 280. Rock complex near the village of Tsarevets, region of Vratsa. Comprises about 40 natural or artificially shaped rock niches and caves in the cliffs rising on the bank of river Iskar. In these niches archaeologists have found about 30 separate inscriptions from different time periods together with hundreds of pictures depicting animals, people, hunting scenes, cult symbols and 'grids' or 'table-shaped paintings'. The palaeographic and language specifics of the inscriptions have allowed experts to date them to the period of 16th – 18th century AD but the pictures and images were made in an earlier period, 7th – 9th century AD. However, the archaic style of some of these suggests that they may be even older. One thing is indisputable though: the complex was inhabited in the course of more than thousand years and was an important cult centre.

276

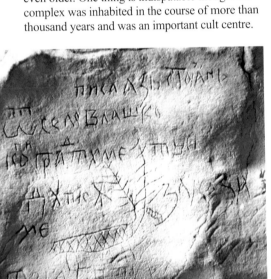

277 278

279 280

281 - 286. Vratsa. The city is located at the foot of Vratsa divide of Stara Planina Mountains. Two residential and defence towers from 17th century: the Tower of Meshchiite and the Tower of Kurtpashovtsi; a renaissance-ethnographic complex including the 18th-century church 'Vaznesenie' (The Ascension); the picturesque gorge 'Vratsata'; the history park 'Hristo Botev' at the place Okolchitsa; the natural park 'Vratsa Balkan'; the cave Ledenika adapted for tourist visits – are among the most interesting tou-rist sites in and around Vratsa.

281

282

283

284

285

286

287 - 291. Vidin: originally the town was built in the 3rd century BC as a Celtic settlement on the Danube riverside and had played at that time an important role in Bulgaria's political and economic life. After 1360 AD it was for some time the capital of an independent Bulgarian kingdom and even after the fall of Bulgaria under the Ottoman rule and until 17th century it was called the main city of Bulgaria. There are well-preserved interesting historical sights: a medieval Bulgarian fortress /4/, the mausoleum of the first after the Liberation Bulgarian Exarch Antim I /2/, the cross-shaped barracks /3/, the gates of the Vidin fortified system from 17th – 18th century /3/ and the mosque and the library of Osman Pazvantoglu /5/ - the Turkish military leader of Northwest Bulgaria around the end of 18th century, the churches 'Sveta Petka' dated 1633 and 'Sveti Panteleymon' of 1634…

287

288 289

290 291

292

293   294

292 - 295. Albutin Rock Monastery near the village of Gra-
dets, region of Vidin. Worshipping by Thracians of the holy
rock and the ancestors has preserved till our time an interesting rite: on the second day of
Easter hundreds of people from
neighbouring villages crowd
there to render homage to their
deceased relatives and friends.
In line with the tradition of the
spirit-protector Heros everyone
carries a portrait of his dear
deceased and joins the ritual
collective dance – the horo –
together with it "to let the dead
dance to their hearts content".

295

296 - 299. The Etropole Monastery 'Sveta Troitsa' (the Holy Trinity) named also 'Varovitets' is located at 5 km east of the town of Etropole in a picturesque place on the northern slopes of Stara Planina Mountains. The monastery is thought to have been founded in 12th century. From a notice left in the beadroll, kept since 1648 we have learned that the monastery was already in existence during the Second Bulgarian State and later had developed into the biggest literary centre in North Bulgaria becoming widely known as the 'Varovitets literary school'. At a distance of 100 m from the monastery is the nice Varovitets waterfall whose water gushes forth from a nearby big karst spring.

300 - 304. Troyan Monastery 'Ouspenie Bogorodichno' (The Assumption) is a functioning, male, stavropygial (i.e. under the direct jurisdiction

296

298

297   299

of the Holy Synod) monks' community and is the third biggest monastery – after Rila and Bachkovo Monasteries – in Bulgaria. Annals dated 1835 tell that the monastery was founded in 1600 by the abbot Kalist. The contemporary mural decoration was made in 1847-1849 by the town of Samokov iconographer Zakhary Zograf, while the gilded iconostasis, whose style characteristics have revealed that it pertains to the Tryavna woodcarvers' school has been carved out in 1839-1840 by Nikola Mateev.

300

301   302

303   304

305 - 312. Etara: an open-air museum of architecture and ethnography. Represents the one and only collection of folk technological devices and facilities powered by water in Bulgaria; the purpose of making their functioning copies was to preserve both the facilities' original type and make as well as the principle on which their design and construction was based. These devices and facilities are exhibited on the river Sivek's right bank and demonstrate technical solutions for using running water as a motive

305

306   307

power. The museum has also a street with artisans' shops- actually it is a whole complex of residential buildings with special premises where the crafts and trade are practised. There, the visitor can see how different articles are manufactured, can get familiar with the particular technology and the specific tools. Not less interesting are the items of public function that are shown there: the town clock tower, double-vault or single-vault bridges, stone fountains for tap water, an inn and catering establishments.

308

309   310

311   312

313

314

313 - 319. Lovech: founded as a Thracian settlement, becoming subsequently a Roman road station Melta, the town kept on growing and developing and during the Middle Ages became an important economic and educational centre. Above the town rise the walls of the medieval town Lovats. In 1187 after a 3-month lasting unsuccessful siege the Byzantine was forced to sign the Lovech peace treaty by which it formally recognised the formation of the Second Bulgarian State. Below the walls of Lovats lies the old district Varosha – at present a reserve of architecture and history – with its houses in tiers upon tiers on the right bank of river Osam. The reserve has more than 160 houses with architecture typical for the second Bulgarian Renaissance. They are two-storey with basement of stone masonry and bay-window-type wooden upper floor(s). Houses are decorated with carved wood, while their yards are closed behind tall stone walls. Of definite interest are the two churches built

in 1834: 'The Assumption' – with an iconoctasis of carved wood, Tryavna school and 'Sveta Nedelya' (The Holy Sabbath) – with murals made after the Debar iconographic school. Here is the only covered bridge in Bulgaria, erected by the master-builder Kolyo Ficheto (Nikola Fichev) in the period of 1872-1874. An 86-m long and 10-m wide wooden structure was built on 7 stone piers; with 64 small shops and artisans' workshops located on both sides of the lane …

315

316   317

318   319

320

321

322

320 - 322. Razgrad: located on the riverside of Beli Lom river on the northern slope of the Razgrad Heights. A city of ancient history as an heir of a Thracian (of an unknown name), a Roman (Abritus) and Bulgarian medieval (Hrazgrad) settlements. Sights to be seen: Ahmed Bey Mosque (1442); Ibrahim Pasha Mosque (1614) – the second biggest in Bulgaria after the city of Shoumen's Tomboul Mosque, which in itself is a unique monument of culture with valuable frescoes and inscriptions; the Clock Tower (1764) about which the Danish engineer Karsten Nibour who had visited Razgrad in 1767 wrote: "On June 22, by 5.30 pm I arrived in Razgrad. As I have not seen in Egypt, Arabia, India and all over Turkey from the Bosporus to the Balkan any clock on a tower, at last here in Razgrad I found one"; the church 'Sveti Nikola'; the Ethnographic complex in the town district of Varosha; the reserve of archaeology 'Abritus', etc.

323 - 326. The ethnographic complex in the district of Varosha in Razgrad: presents the most attractive and typical features of the life, ideas, beliefs and custom-ritual system of the ethnic group called 'kapantsi'. Their life traditions and customs are rather ancient and it is believed that they are direct descendants of the Proto-Bulgarian ethnic group

323

325

324   326

327 - 331. Abritus: an ancient city founded by the Romans in 1st century AD. In 251 AD, in a battle Romans and Goths fought not far from the town, the Roman Emperor Decius died and in the reign of Byzantine Emperor Justinian I (527-565) its fortified walls were thoroughly reconstructed and strengthened. Excavations have revealed remains of 3 towers, part of the fortified wall and of a big residential building; in a lapidary nearby about 60 ethnographic monuments and architectural details from Roman times until 19th century are exhibited

327

328

329

330

331

332 - 336. Ethnographic complex in the village of Topchii, region of Razgrad: comprises several Kapan houses and the yards between them as well as their interior where an interesting ethnographic collection is exhibited

332

333

334

335   336

337

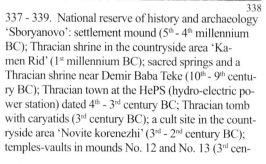

338

339

337 - 339. National reserve of history and archaeology 'Sboryanovo': settlement mound (5th - 4th millennium BC); Thracian shrine in the countryside area 'Kamen Rid' (1st millennium BC); sacred springs and a Thracian shrine near Demir Baba Teke (10th - 9th century BC); Thracian town at the HePS (hydro-electric power station) dated 4th - 3rd century BC; Thracian tomb with caryatids (3rd century BC); a cult site in the countryside area 'Novite korenezhi' (3rd - 2nd century BC); temples-vaults in mounds No. 12 and No. 13 (3rd century BC), more than 100 burial mounds grouped in several mound necropolises (2nd-1st millennium BC); impressive megalithic constructions in the countryside area 'Tainstveniya grad' (the mysterious town) - not dated yet; the monastery Demir Baba Teke (16th century AD); oral and written data indicating the likely location somewhere in the area of Dausdava (the City of Wolves), pointed out by the Roman cartographer Claudius Ptolemeus in his map NONA EUROPA TABULA or the polis Helis of the Gettan rulers. Thus, in short, is how

'Sboryanovo' looks: one of the most important cult centres of ancient Thrace .

340 - 341. Thracian tomb in the national reserve of history and archaeology 'Sboryanovo' near the village of Sveshtari, region of Razgrad, 3rd century BC, of a Gettan ruler and his wife. Consists of a dromos (corridor) and three chambers. The central chamber of the vault is decorated with caryatids: female sculptured figures, while a delicate picture represents the deification of the ruler. Because of its unique architecture, sculptural and painted decoration the vault has been entered UNESCO's List of the World Cultural and Natural Heritage Sites

340

341

342

343

344

342 - 349. The rock monastery not far from the village
of Ivanovo, 13th - 14th century
AD. The monastery complex
near the village of Ivanovo,
region of Rousse was built
with the financial and other
support from Tsar Ivan-Assen
II (1218-1241 AD). Monastic
cells have been grouped around
7 churches and chapels. The
oldest section of the monastery
comprises the monks' cells
around the 'Buried church' and
the 'Baptismal house'. They are
distinguished by their smooth
and carefully hewn walls and
are connected to each other

345

346

by a system of paths and stairs. This is the Archangel Michael Monastery. The second group of monastic cells are centred around the church 'The Lord's vale' and still further east is the complex around the 'Demolished church'.

To the southwest from the countryside area 'Pismata' is 'The Church' - the best preserved part of the monastery complex. In both parts of the rock church scores of evangelic scenes, most of them episodes from the Sufferings of Christ (Passional of Lord), and on the narthex's north wall is the donor's portrait of Tsar Ivan-Alexander (1331-1371): an explicit proof that the Tsar has given his support to the monks' cloister. Due to its exceptional artistic value the murals in the Ivanovo rock monastery have been assessed as a step of its own in the development of the 16th century European culture and have been entered UNESCO' List of the World Cultural and Natural Heritage Sites

348

347   349

350 - 353. The rock monastery 'Sveti Dimiter Basarbovski' (Saint Dimiter from Basarbovo): hewn in the cliffs by the village of Basarbovo, region of Rousse in the 15th century, at present is the only functioning rock monastery where services and liturgies glorifying God are held every day. In the monastery's book of chronicles there is a marginal note written by the hand of Romanian Patriarch Justinian about his visit to the monastery in 1953.

350

351

352

353

354 - 357. More than 1000 rock churches and monastic cells are known by now in Bulgaria. Hewn in cliffs at a height varying from a couple of metres to 70 m above the ground, many of them being inaccessible without special equipment. This is the reason to have in many of them well-preserved pictures, inscriptions and murals of inestimable historical and artistic value.
An epitaph at the entrance to a rock church near the village of Krepcha, region of Targovishte, the earliest Old-Bulgarian inscription, 10th century AD

354

355   356

357

358. Fortress wall encircling the medieval town of Dristra (modern Silistra) which accommodated the see of the Bulgarian patriarch in the reign of Tsar Symeon (893-927) and Tsar Peter (927-970)

359. Late antique tomb discovered at Silistra; fourth century AD

358

359

360. The cliff at Assenova krepost (Assen's castle) with an inscription on it, the gist of which is: "In the 6739 from the Creation (=1231 AD), Indiction 4, the man elevated by God, Ivan Assen II, Tsar of the Bulgarians and the Greeks, as well as of the other states, installed as governor Alexis the Sevast (Sebastos) and fortified this castle".

361. Assenova krepost (Assen's castle) - medieval fortified settlement, stretching over an area of 15 decares (1.5 ha); 11th - 14th century; Assenovgrad, Plovdiv region

362. Floating ice on the Danube, the river that is the state border between Bulgaria and Romania. It is relatively seldom to observe an icebound Danube as the winter is not that bleak every year.

360

361

363 - 367. Rousse: the largest Bulgarian city on the Danube riverside. Archaeologists have studied the so-called 'Rousse settlement mound' located within the limits of the contemporary city. It was found that it is more than 5000 years old: the earliest documented traces of communal life at that place. In 1st century AD the ancient town of Sextaginta Prista (the Sixty Ships) was established and it should be noted that 'prista' means a specific type of Greek patrol ship. The settlement was probably founded by the Roman Emperor Vespasian (69-79 AD) and existed until 4th century AD when the Avars destroyed it. In 14th century according to the written traditions of this town a settlement named Rossi has been mentioned, while in 19th century the city under the name of Rouschouk had become administrative centre of the Danube Region (Touna vilaet) of the Ottoman Empire, comprising territories belonging today to three separate states: Serbia, Romania and Bulgaria.

363

364

For decades Rousse has been the first Bulgarian city of definitely European appearance: over 200 buildings have entered the golden fund of Rousse's architectural heritage, the best known being 'Dohodno Zdanie' built in 1902, a work of the architects Raul-Paul Brank, Georg Lang and Frank Stoltz. Another symbol of Rousse is the monument of Liberty erected in 1908 by the Florentine architect and sculptor Arnoldo Dzocchi. The writer Elias Kanetti, a Nobel Prize winner for literature for 1981, born in Rousse in 1905 wrote: "If all windows that became open before me in my youth were in Vienna, then with the help of Isaac Babel I perceived that Rouschouk was the first window I had lent over to observe all races, to listen to all languages, to study all the traditions, to become familiar with all the nations which anyway did quite well together in this microcosm."

365

366   367

369

368 - 371. Bulgarian Black
Sea Coast: with its broad
sand beaches, warm seawater,
with its tender climate and
innumerable romantic corners
possesses an irresistible
attractive power

370

371

372

373 374

372 - 375. Varna: the biggest Bulgarian city on the Black Sea Coast. The earliest significant traces of communal life within the city limits are from Varna's halcolithic /Copper Age/ necropolis, dated by the end of the 5ᵗʰ millennium BC, where the Varna treasure was discovered. It consists of 3100 gold articles with a total weight of 6.5 kg and among them are the earliest in the world symbols of power: 2 gold sceptres. In 6ᵗʰ century BC Hellenic colonists have established here a town known under the name of Odessos, which after 7ᵗʰ century AD was renamed by the Slavs Varna. It took a place in the European history in 1444 with the defeat of the liberation crusade against the Turks led by the Polish-Hungarian king Vladislav III Jagelo. He was killed in the battle of Varna and remained in history as Vladislav Varnenchik (i.e. 'of Varna'). Among the many noteworthy sights in the city of Varna are the Roman Thermae, the biggest public building of antiquity in Bulgaria, erected by the end of the 2ⁿᵈ century AD as well as the city cathedral 'The Assumption', erected in 1885.

376

377

376 - 378. Aladzha Monastery: a rock monastery not far from the city of Varna, established probably in 12th century AD. Its name means 'variegated' in Turkish and has obviously something to do with the murals with which its walls were covered in 14th century. Nearby, on the same cliffs, there is another complex, called the Catacombs, which was found to have existed as early as in the 4th century AD and had been related with early Christianity

378

379 - 383. The reserve of archaeology 'Yaylata' near the village of Kamen Bryag, region of Dobrich: a prolonged seaside rock terrace that has formed during the slide of a large rock massif and in whose cliffs scores of artificial caves were dug and had been used in different historical times as family tombs by the local Gettan population, as shrines, cave dwellings and churches. In most general terms they had been in use for more than 2500 years and in one of the rock churches there were regular liturgies until 1940.

379

380   381

382   383

384

384. The Magic spring: one of the Devnya karst springs near the town of Devnya, region of Varna. Not far from it are the remains of the Roman town of Marcianopolis, founded by Emperor Trajanus in 106 AD, which had been the scene of important historical events until 7th century when it was finally destroyed by the Avars and abandoned.

385. The Upright Stones: a fantastic fossil stone forest spreading on an area of about 50 sq.-km between Varna and Devnya. It has been assumed that the area has strong energy emanation; declared as a natural landmark as early as in 1937 it enjoys considerable tourist interest

385

386

388

387 - 388. Nature reserve
'Kaliakra': covers part of the
peninsula of the same name, the
only Bulgarian nature reserve
comprising also part of the
sea shelf. Established as early
as in 1941 as a people's park
and since 1960 assigned to the
category of nature reserves
in order to protect the habitat
of the Monk Seal as well as
the breeding grounds of rare
and threatened with extinction
species of birds. On the
peninsula proper the Thracian
fortress of Terizis was built as
early as in the 6th century BC.
It had existed until 12th century
AD under different names:
Akra and Akra Castellum

387

389

390

389 - 395. Nesebar:
ancient settlement in which
communal life has not ceased
for almost 4000 years;
today declared as a reserve
of architecture and history,
entered UNESCO's List of the
World Cultural and Natural
Heritage Sites. Founded by
the Thracians (Menabria)
in the 2nd millennium BC,
later had become a Doric
colony (Mesabria), until 8th
century AD being a part of
the Byzantine Empire and
since 812 AD was annexed
by Khan Kroum and became
part of the Bulgarian State.

391

392

393

394

Its heyday was in 14th century under the rule of
Tsar Ivan-Alexander. On the relatively small area
of the peninsula 41 churches were revealed, the
oldest of them dated 5th century AD. Some 80
houses have been preserved in the town from
the time of the Bulgarian Renaissance (17th - 19th
century), pertaining to the so-called type of Nesebar
houses. They are closed town houses, normally
two-storey and demonstrate the rich residential
culture of the local population from that time. In a
very close vicinity to Nesebar is the resort complex
Slanchev Bryag (the Sunny Beach) - one of the
most renowned and frequented seaside resorts in
Bulgaria, with excellent climate and a beach strip of
up to 150-m width.

395

396

397

396 - 398. The antique tomb-mausoleum near the town of Pomorie, region of Bourgas, dated 3rd-4th century AD. A corridor of 22-m length and a central round room have been preserved. In the centre of the room there is hollow column like a mushroom towards the top. The corridor ceiling is an arch merging with the central column: a unique architectural solution - a return to an old Thracian burial tradition.

398

399

400

401

399 - 401. The island 'Sveta Anastasia', a small rocky island at 3 nautical miles east of the city of Bourgas. In the past there was a monastery, 'Sveta Anastasia", whose 17th century church is still well-preserved today

402

403 404

405 406

407   408

409   410

402 - 410. Bourgas: the city has spread on part of
the seashore around the Bay of Bourgas. To the
east it borders on the Black Sea, while from the
the mainland it is surrounded by three large lakes:
Mandra, Vaya and Atanasovsko. Bourgas has come
up into being relatively recently, in 17th century
AD but today it is the second biggest city on the
coast (after Varna) and the fourth biggest one in the
country after Sofia, Plovdiv and Varna. A city of
abundant green vegetation and wonderful Seaside
Park, a lot of sunny days and nice beach with darkly
coloured rich in magnetite sand. Two churches: the
cathedral temple of 'Sveti Kiril and Metodiy' and
'The Mother of God' deserve closer attention, while
the art gallery offers to the inquisitive eye a number
of works by local artists, masters from the country
and a rich collection of icons… Another noteworthy
sight is the Bourgas Thermae, highly valued in
ancient times - by the mineral spring there were
Roman thermae as early as in 4th century AD.

411 - 418. Atanasovsko Lake: a hyperhaline lake by the Black Sea coast almost within the city. Its depth varies from 30 to 80 cm and it is a unique combination of wild nature and human economic activities. Annually the saltworks on the lake produces between 40,000 and 70,000 tonnes of sea-salt. Of the 400 species of birds of the Bulgarian avifauna, 315 occur here and 62 of them breed in or around the lake; of the 100 species of birds in the Red Book of Bulgaria 86 have been recorded here. Above the lake goes the Via Pontica migratory flyway.

411

412   413

414

415

416

417

The lake has been declared a managed reserve and is one of the 10 wetlands in Bulgaria that have been entered the Ramsar Convention List of Wetlands with International Importance. The most visited place in Bulgaria both by professional ornithologists and by groups for specialised tourism from all over Europe: more than 50,000 people a year.

On the river Ropotamo Managed reserve Arkoutino within the limits of the natural park Ropotamo south of Sozopol

418

419

420

419 - 426. Sozopol: a town located on a not very big peninsula, rivalling Nesebar with its picturesque situation. The first human presence here has been dated by the 4th millennium BC, the settlement then consisting of pile dwellings. The everyday material culture of the population of the 2nd millennium BC indicates it was already a Thracian one and belonged to the tribe of Skirmians. In 611 BC Greek settlers have founded on the peninsula a polis (city-state) called Apolonia, since 330 AD it is within the borders of the Byzantine Empire and was renamed Sozopol (the Saved Town). After 812 it was annexed to the Bulgarian State by Khan Kroum.

421

Today more than 100 buildings erected in 18th and 19th century AD have been preserved in Sozopol's old town. These are 2- and 3-storey houses built of stone and wood. Usually their ground floors have been used as storerooms for fishermen's equipment, farming implements and wine casks, while on the upper one or two floors were the living rooms. The typical silhouette of the houses with upper floors standing out and overhanging the narrow cobbled streets that lead right to the seashore gives the town somewhat renaissance charm. The five wonderful beaches attract in summer scores of thousands of holiday-makers

422

423   424

425   426

427. Windsurfing is one of the favourite pastime for thousand of holiday-makers on the Bulgarian Black Sea coast

428. The ski runs below the summits Golyam and Malak Markoudzhik in the resort of Borovets in Rila Mountain offer excellent environment for skiing and snowboarding.

429. Winter in the Pirin National Park

430. Herds of game in the Loudogorie, a plateau in the eastern part of the Myzian Plain with an average altitude of 300 m. Scarred by the canyons of several rivers it still has extensive remains of the onetime oak forests called Wild Woods (Louda Gora or Deliorman).

431. The Chaira Lakes: a group of landslide lakes in Rodopi Mountains, near the village of Trigrad, region of Smolyan

432. City of Veliko Tarnovo and the hill of Tsarevets: a general view. The Constantinople Patriarch Kalist wrote about the city in 14th century: "… Tarnovo, which is for Bulgarians the regal city and second in importance by words and deeds after Tsarigrad (Constantinople)"

433. A karst canyon, river Vit valley, village of Sadovets

43

431

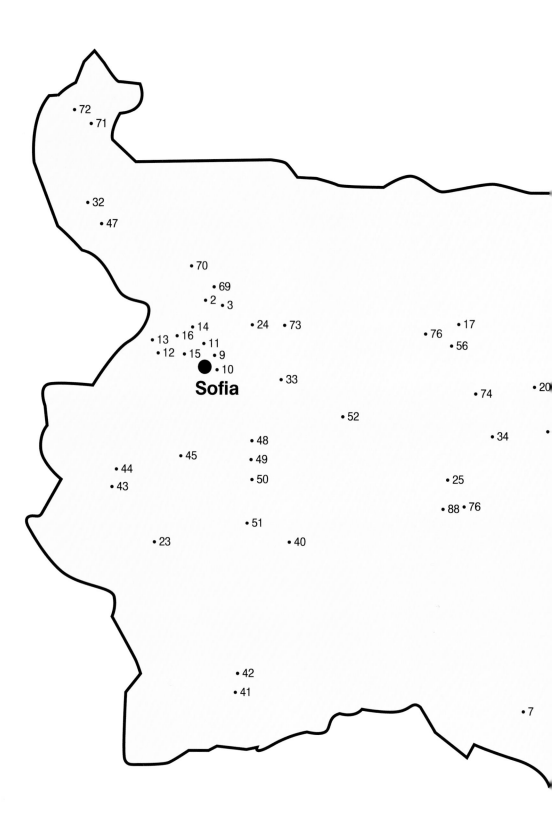

Sofia

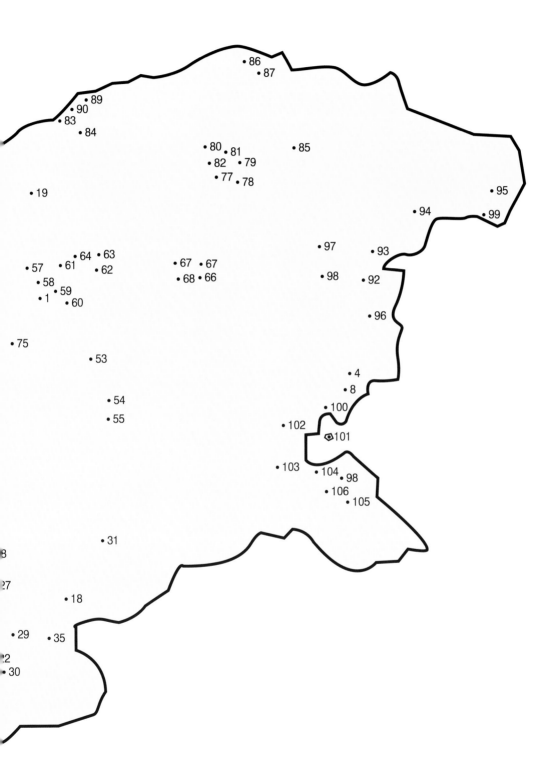

189

List of sites included in the book

The Little Gift Book of
BULGARIA
with 433 colour illustrations

Autor of the foreword: Hristo Bukovski
Editor of the Bulgarian Text: Vyara Kandjeva
Photos: Vyara Kandjeva, Antoniy Handjiysky,
Graphic design: Antoniy Handjiysky
English Translation: Vladimir Pomakov

Scanning and imagesetting: BULGED Ltd., Sofia
Preprint and Layout: GED Ltd., Sofia

Borina Publishing House
E-mail: borina@borina.com
www.borina.com

ISBN 954 500 114 3

Printed in the Czech Republic